LOVE GOOD FOOD

Easy-to-Cook, Stylish Recipes Inspired by Modern Flavors

LOVE GOOD FOOD

Easy-to-Cook, Stylish Recipes Inspired by Modern Flavors

SOPHIE MICHELL

DUNCAN BAIRD PUBLISHERS

LONDON

LOVE GOOD FOOD
Sophie Michell

Distributed in the USA and Canada by
Sterling Publishing Co., Inc.
387 Park Avenue South
New York, NY 10016-8810

First published in the United Kingdom and Ireland in
2012 by
Duncan Baird Publishers Ltd
Sixth Floor, Castle House
75–76 Wells Street
London W1T 3QH

Managing Editor: Grace Cheetham
Editors: Alison Bolus and Camilla Davis
Americanizer: Norma MacMillan
Managing Designer: Manisha Patel
Designer: Gail Jones
Production: Uzma Taj
Commissioned photography: Toby Scott
Food Stylist: Jayne Cross
Prop Stylist: Tamsin Weston

Library of Congress Cataloging-in-Publication
Data available

ISBN: 978-1-84899-014-2

10 9 8 7 6 5 4 3 2 1

Typeset in Lisboa
Colour reproduction by XY Digital
Printed in China by Imago

For information about custom editions, special sales,
premium and corporate purchases, please contact
Sterling Special Sales Department at 800-805-5489 or
specialsales@sterlingpub.com.

Acknowledgements

Thank you to all the team at DBP, to my agents at Deborah
Mckenna and to my family for being so wonderful.

Publisher's note

While every care has been taken in compiling the recipes
for this book, Duncan Baird Publishers, or any other
persons who have been involved in working on this
publication, cannot accept responsibility for any errors
or omissions, inadvertent or not, that may be found in
the recipes or text, nor for any problems that may arise
as a result of preparing one of these recipes. If you are
pregnant or breastfeeding or have any special dietary
requirements or medical conditions, it is advisable to
consult a medical professional before following any of the
recipes contained in this book.

Notes on the Recipes

Unless otherwise stated:
Use large eggs, and medium fruit and vegetables
Use fresh ingredients, including herbs and chilies
1 tsp. = 5ml   1 tbsp. = 15ml   1 cup = 240ml

To my grandmother, Ruth Hughes

Contents

Introduction

I have wanted to write this book for years. For me, food is all about love—love of the ingredients you can work with, the different cuisines and techniques that you can use, the tastes, textures and aromas you can serve up and the memories you can create.

These days we are bombarded with visions of food and chefs all the time: in magazines and books, and on websites and TV. Chefs create such amazing dishes in an instant, but we know that behind the scenes they have an army of minions and a huge, well-stocked professional kitchen supporting them. Yet despite knowing that, we long to achieve what they achieve, preferably with effortless ease. It is possible to make amazing dishes on your own at home—and I hope to show you that cooking is a fantastic and enjoyable way to spend your time. Cooking for family and friends is often one of the best ways of bringing people together. What could be more enjoyable than sharing good food, wine and conversation around the table?

MY BACKGROUND

I started working in kitchens aged 15, although for as long as my family can remember I had my head in cookbooks and my hands working with food. Since then I've worked in a great variety of professional kitchens, including some amazing high-end restaurants, some with Michelin-starred kitchens, where the cooking is like a form of alchemy. This is the most polished and perfect food you are ever likely to eat.

For the past 10 years, though, I have not always had the luxury of a professional kitchen behind me. During that time I have cooked for many events on location or have served up food on film sets, where the conditions can be primitive, to say the least. However, these less-than-perfect conditions do not mean that these clients haven't all wanted good restaurant-style food... I just have to simplify my recipes to work in smaller environments and challenging conditions. At the other end of the scale, I have also cooked in private homes for the rich and famous in situations that bring their own, quite different, challenges.

This book is the result of my experience. It is full of beautiful and stunning recipes, written simply and plainly. There are no complicated terms and no difficult cheffy techniques, which can just as easily put people off as impress them. Inevitably, the recipes vary in the skill and time required to make them. While some may need only a handful of ingredients, others require more. But they are all dishes that will be loved by everyone.

I am not pretending that this is a "ready in 30 minutes" type book, because many of the recipes are more complex than that. Also, I do want to stretch people's imaginations a bit, as in the recipes for Tomato & Geranium Gelatins with Crab & Micro Basil (see page 64), Summer Vegetable & Truffle-Oil Pizzas (see page 130) and the Smoked Tea- & Star-Anise-Braised Pork Ribs with Pickled Cucumber (see page 96), for example. I also want to take the mystique out of ingredients such as pea shoots, sumac and truffle oil, so that you are happy to use them when you cook at home.

COOKING AND EATING MY WAY AROUND THE WORLD

This book also reflects the other love of my life, apart from cooking, which is traveling. This has always been intertwined with my career in food. Throughout my travels around the world, I have discovered amazing dishes and ingredients.

Babi guling in Bali...

When I was 11, my family traveled around Bali and Australia for 8 months. I come from a very foodie background, but this is where my eyes were really opened to a whole new world of food. I could not get over things like the lurid pink tapioca desserts sold on the roadside, the aroma of chicken satay being grilled or the fact that the hotel pet monkey would pick us green coconuts to drink from.

We devoured our way through Bali: coconut-banana pancakes with palm sugar for breakfast or *babi guling* (slow-roasted spiced suckling pig) in Ubud, next door to a dark temple with frangipani and incense heavy in the air... Then later we'd have salty coconut-oil fries after swimming with spinner dolphins on the volcanic sandy beaches of Lovina, or eat plates of dangerous barracuda (now spiced and grilled), which we had chased in the sea while snorkeling that morning. I have never forgotten those vibrant experiences.

Kangaroo steaks in Australia...

The magic continued in Australia. Where else could you find sushi, sashimi and miso soup next to fluffy pancakes and bacon on a hotel breakfast buffet? Bondi Beach was where I had my first oyster. I hated it, and rarely ate them again until I was 19, when I suddenly fell in love with them and would consume them en masse while working in a fish restaurant in London.

We also tried kangaroo steaks and loved them, then went on to experience the best Mexican, Greek and Italian food in Melbourne (think steaming authentic fresh cilantro- and lime-laced burritos, cinnamon-scented homemade moussakas and perfectly *al dente* spaghetti vongole...).

These travels subconsciously developed my love of combining flavors from different cultures, which is something that Australian chefs in particular do so well. In this book, I want to show simple ways of cooking in this style. It can be a risky business mixing different food cultures together, but I love it when it is done properly. This is where dishes such as the Asian Beef Carpaccio with Micro Herbs (see page 46), which mixes Italian and Southeast Asian flavors, or the Sesame Tuna with Wasabi Potato Salad & Pink Grapefruit Dressing (see page 49) are highlights.

Polenta uncia and *sopressa* in Italy...

Years later, back in Europe, I spent months on and off in Milan, Como and Monza in Italy, learning how to make proper Italian food at home, with an Italian mama. This is the best way to learn Italian cooking. Then I spent much of the rest of my time discovering the hidden restaurant gems in the area, learning even more. Each restaurant would specialize in one dish, so off we would go for platters of smoked cheese and pancetta risotto oozing off our forks or to a bio-farm restaurant with the best tagliata (rare steak). On another day, we would drive up into the mountains for *polenta uncia* (polenta fried with garlic, cheese, butter and sage) and roasted rabbit, followed by shots of grappa. The fried polenta used here in the Venison Steaks with Pickled Red Cabbage & Truffle-Polenta Fries (see page 112) is an adaptation of this.

In Aslo (just north of Venice), I discovered homemade *sopressa* (cured pork sausage) with mustard fruits (which star in the Ham Hock Terrine with Mustard Fruits on page 36) as well as wonderful local cheeses. On the way to Lake Garda, it was pumpkin and amaretti raviolis followed by grilled trout fresh from the water. Beta-carotene-rich pumpkin and other winter squashes are a staple part of our diet and show no sign of losing their continuing starring role. Try squash in the Butternut Squash, Chili & Maple Syrup Soup (see page 28). I would often return home with a suitcase full of fresh porcini mushrooms, which I found far more interesting to pack than the fashionable shoes from Milan. Similarly, using Pecorino Sardo cheese in pesto is something I picked up when consulting for a cooking school in Sardinia.

Boureki and Sfakian cheese pies in Crete...

Ten years ago, my family moved to Crete. Greek food is hugely under-appreciated, but we ate really well there. It is a simple diet that relies on fresh seasonal produce. It hasn't really changed much over the centuries and is often hailed as the healthiest diet of the Med. This is where I first tried sea urchins, with their sweet iodine flavor, served chilled with lemon and olive oil. I made *boureki* (zucchini layered with mint, mizithra and tomato) at my friends' taverna, and discovered air-dried octopus, Sfakian cheese pies, chestnut stifado and braised wild greens with artichokes. Our renovated old house was the central village house and, in the old Kafenion tradition, still has an ancient wood-burning bread oven and grape pit. I was often transported back in time when sitting in the dappled sunlight in our ancient-vine-covered courtyard. You could feel that it had seen many a celebration dinner with friends and family.

Fattoush and *za'atar* breads in Beirut...

Then recently, I spent a year in Beirut, consulting for a restaurant, which is where I learned about the most romantic of flavors, such as rosewater, orange blossom, pomegranate, pistachio and sumac. These aromatic and jewel-like additions are part of my everyday cooking now in recipes such as Sea Bass Sashimi with Pomegranate & Micro Herbs (see page 52). I love the Lebanese mezze style of eating. *Fattoush*, pomegranate-caramelized chicken livers, baby birds, *hindbi* (wild chicory with fried onions), grilled halloumi, beet houmous, *shish taouk* (juicy chicken kebabs) and many beautiful lamb dishes were all served up and loved. Beets are a more versatile root vegetable than you might have thought. In addition to being used in houmous, I have used it to make a mousse (see page 75) and also borrowed its fantastic color for the most stunning gravlax: Beet-Cured Salmon Gravlax (see page 56). This is one of those dishes that is almost too beautiful to eat. Food becomes seriously fun when you start experimenting like this. As for exciting ingredients such as *za'atar*, I started using it when I learned to make breads in the Beiruti mountains.

LEARNING TO EXPERIMENT

People are often scared of the unknown, and inexperienced cooks will often revert back to the tried and tested methods and ingredients that they feel safe with. This is especially so when entertaining, because taking a chance on a new recipe containing unusual ingredients when you have guests coming might seem to be tempting fate. However, it is worth taking the plunge once in a while, because when you master a new skill or really taste a new ingredient and learn how it can come into your daily life, it opens up a world of new ideas and creations. Similarly, be prepared to change—try adding an ingredient to a familiar dish and see what happens. This is how I created the Blood Orange Tart (see page 166), the Caramelized Coconut-Rice Pudding (see page 154) and Pimm's Trifle (see page 156). For a savory example, consider the Sour Cherry Meatballs with Buttery Tagliatelli on page 102. Always popular, meatballs are now appearing on menus everywhere, whether on their own with vegetables, in a sauce or in a pasta or rice dish, and it is so easy to make them exciting and unusual by adding some new ingredients, such as the sour cherries and pine nuts that I chose to use in the recipe.

Trying new or simply unfamiliar ingredients can be nerve-wracking: investing money in an unknown product and not understanding how to use it can seem like a risk. I am sure we all have the odd pot of obscure spice or vinegar that we used for one recipe and never picked up again. However, it is only through experimenting that we develop our cooking skills and expand our repertoire, and in so doing learn to take the courage to be inventive. I am hoping that once you have tried some of the ingredients I have featured in this book, they will become part of your everyday cooking.

Here are some of the vegetables you might like to try: **Celery root** is wonderful mashed (see page 205) if you fancy a change from potato. Not only is it low in carbohydrate, but it has a wonderful savory flavor and is very versatile. **Fennel** is much underrated: it lends a subtle aniseed flavor to dishes such as Five-Spice Scallops with Fennel Purée & Orange Dressing (see page 61). **Chestnuts** are perfect for giving a dish a taste of winter. Try the Pork, Quince & Chestnut Casserole with Watercress Mash (see page 95) for the ultimate in comfort food on cold winter days. **Jerusalem artichokes** are quite unappealing to look at, but they make the most amazing soups and roasts. Their flavor is similar to that of globe artichokes, and they are great during the fall and winter months. Try them in the Jerusalem Artichoke Soup with Sourdough-Parmesan Croûtons (see page 29) and Chicken Breast with Hazelnut & Jerusalem Artichoke Couscous (see page 83). **Swiss chard** is a leafy vegetable with either white or multicolored stems. These greens make a change from the usual cabbage or spinach. Finally, **quince** is an old-fashioned fruit that is inedible

in its raw state, but when cooked is wonderfully fragrant and deep pink. I love making jams and chutneys with it, but I also add it to savory dishes, such as the Pork, Quince & Chestnut Casserole with Watercress Mash (see page 95).

Many of the more unusual storecupboard ingredients you will find in the recipes are there as a result of my travels. Since living in Beirut I have adopted a few ingredients that will always be in my pantry:

Pomegranate molasses is a syrup that I now use in preference to aged balsamic vinegar. It adds a little bit of both sweetness and sourness to dishes. It is great with lemon juice and olive oil in salad dressings; it glazes meat; and it also adds balance to casseroles and rice dishes. I have used it to give a wonderful flavor to the Halloumi, Quinoa, Pomegranate & Mint Salad (see page 67).

Za'atar is a wonderful Middle-Eastern mixture of herbs and spices. It changes its recipe according to the region, but mine is the classic Lebanese mix of toasted sesame seeds, dried thyme, fresh thyme, sumac, sea salt and pepper. I use za'atar for flavoring breads in the Za'atar Flatbreads (see page 179); mixing with oils or yogurt for dips; and sprinkling on chicken and lamb before cooking. You can make your own mix.

Sumac is actually a small astringent pink berry, not a spice. After drying, it is ground up and can then be sprinkled over salads and various other dishes, adding an almost citrus flavor. I have used it in the Lamb Skewers with Lentil Salad on page 100.

Cassia bark is another spice to try. It is very similar to cinnamon in flavor and in appearance, though it's a touch more spicy and has a hint of musk to it. I love the huge curled bark; it's really beautiful. You can use cinnamon instead if you cannot get hold of it. If you want to experiment with cassia, try the Cassia-Scented Custard Tart with Apple Compote (see page 155).

Rosewater and orange-flower water are the two most romantic and whimsical ingredients in my opinion. Although I have been using them for years, they still transport me straight back to the Middle East, where I can picture myself in the searing heat of a summer's day, cooled only by fresh homemade lemonade mixed with mint leaves, rosewater and crushed ice, or eating orange-scented pastries served after dark during Ramadan. I like to use rosewater in desserts and Persian rice dishes, while orange-flower water adds a wonderful touch to all kinds of sweets. I use it to bring a new dimension to that well-loved favorite, the chocolate éclair, to make the Orange-Blossom Éclairs (see page 184). The result is a delicate and exotic treat.

My time in Italy also introduced me to many new ingredients, some of which have since become firm favorites and will be found in my recipes.

Truffle oil may seem very luxurious, but I highly recommend buying a little bottle of it. Drops of it can transform food. You'll be amazed how much it raises the flavor when added to cauliflower soup, simple mashed potato or risottos... I have used it to great effect in the Venison Steaks with Pickled Red Cabbage & Truffle-Polenta Fries (see page 112) and the Summer Vegetable & Truffle-Oil Pizzas (see page 130).

As for *mostarda di frutta*, or mustard fruits, this is basically a relish or chutney to have with cold cuts, cheese and salamis. This jewel-like condiment consists of whole candied fruits suspended in a sugar syrup that is flavored with mustard oil. It is both beautiful and tasty. You can purchase it in Italian markets, specialty food stores and in some supermarkets as well as online.

LOOKING BACK TO OUR PAST

Many ingredients that were used in times past are now enjoying a new-found popularity. **Spelt** is a great grain to introduce into your diet. It's an ancient form of wheat that is more easily digestible for people with a wheat intolerance. I love the nutty flavor and texture of spelt berries or kernels. They are just lovely when made into a risotto, such as the Spelt & Roasted Butternut Squash Risotto (see page 133): its rounded nuttiness is comfort food at its best.

Quinoa, amaranth and millet, other ancient grains, are making a welcome comeback. Quinoa, much loved by the Aztecs, is a great grain to include in your diet. It is high in protein and contains amino acids and more nutrients than, say, couscous or rice. Plus its flavor and appearance are unique. So try it in the Halloumi, Quinoa, Pomegranate & Mint Salad (see page 67). Try experimenting with grains to see how they will fit into your cooking and what their different qualities are. Trying out new ingredients like this, mixing and matching them with old favorites to create interesting new dishes, is the joy of cooking.

Samphire, or salicornia, is under-used, but it really tastes amazing. It is named after the patron saint of fishermen, Saint Peter, or "Saint Pierre," which evolved into "Sainpierre" and then to "Samphire." It has a great salty, fresh flavor and is also known as "sea asparagus." It is perfect steamed with seafood and served lightly buttered. Look for it in summer at specialty fish merchants. I have used it in the Shrimp & Samphire Tarts (see page 54).

NOT ALL GOOD FOOD HAS TO BE EXPENSIVE

However, this book isn't just about expensive or exotic ingredients. I have made some dishes using cheaper cuts of meat to prove that fantastic food can be made with all sorts of ingredients. One of the less well known cuts is hanger steak, sometimes called butcher's steak, which is very cheap and tasty. In Paris, where it is known as *onglet*, it is usually served as "Steak frites," coming with fries and garlic butter. If marinated, it makes a delicious grilled steak, but it must not be over cooked, because it will become tough. Fresh pork belly, sometimes called pork side, is another flavorsome, budget-conscious favorite that I have glazed with miso in another one of the dishes: Miso-Glazed Pork Belly with Stir-Fried Bok Choy on page 92.

TAKING A MODERN LOOK AT FOOD

The other aspect to this book is to take a modern look at food, which is where micro greens come in. For years it's been the fashion to pile up a mix of micro greens on a plate in restaurants. In fact, micro greens and the flavors they contribute should be handled with more respect than normal salad greens and herbs. They are stronger in taste and can add a powerful punch along with undeniable beauty. Knowing which one is good with the right ingredients is important. Micro greens make a fantastic difference to recipes—try the Herb Consommé (see page 26), Asian Beef Carpaccio with Micro Herbs (see page 46) and Fried Sea Bass with Micro Herb & Bell Pepper Salad (see page 115).

As for pea shoots, with their bright green chlorophyll leaves and delicate fronds, they are great to use in soups, salads and various other dishes. They really are so beautiful to work with and add a fresh spring look to any dish. Also, just see how versatile they are from the following recipes I have used them in: Pea Shoot & Watercress Soup (see page 22), Pea-Shoot Pancakes with Crispy Pancetta & Sweet Chili Sauce (see page 35) and Potato Gnocchi with Pea-Shoot Pesto & Pecorino Shavings (see page 137). All of these dishes have been lifted out of the ordinary by the presence of the pea shoots.

I love dishes that look fresh and clean, such as the Pan-Grilled Shrimp with Mango (see page 129) and the Tomato & Geranium Gelatins with Crab & Micro Basil (see page 64). Simple, but appealing. Also eye-catching, this time because of their bright colors, are dishes such as Pan-Grilled Chicken, Beet, Manchego & Candied Pecan Salad (see page 30) and Spiced Lamb Flatbreads (see page 43). For beauty, Beet-Cured Salmon Gravlax (see page 56) is unbeatable. This dish uses edible flowers, which have been my passion since I was a child: crystallized rose petals, violets, micro-borage flowers, pansies... They all add magic.

My final favorite for extra drama is edible gold, in the form of gold leaf and gold dust or powder, which has garnished dishes in the Middle East and India for some time. These little pots of gilt can be found in cake decorating suppliers, specialty cookware stores and online. They are expensive, but a little goes a long way and they really make an impact. Everything tastes better covered in gold...

NEW TECHNIQUES TO TRY

I want you to learn some new and varied cooking styles in this book, so throughout I have endeavored to show you how to follow techniques that might at first seem complicated, such as making a twice-baked soufflé (see page 76), but are in fact straightforward. Once you've mastered the techniques, all the dishes will be within your grasp. In the light meals chapter, I show you how to clarify a stock and make a consommé (see page 26), and these techniques can be applied to lots of different flavors and clear soups. I also show you how to make a terrine (see page 36). Terrines are a joy to make and very simple. I love the unveiling and slicing of a new terrine, and they come into their own for celebration dinners. In addition, I show you how to make ceviche (see page 53), where the fish is cured by the citrus juices, and cure salmon (see page 56). In the the main meals chapter I show you how to cook the perfect risotto (see page 133); make your own ravioli (see page 134) and gnocchi (see page 137); and prepare light-as-a-feather tempura (see page 139). Moving on to sweet dishes, in the desserts chapter I show you how to make the perfect egg custard (see page 156). Finally, we move to the baking chapter, where you will learn how to make choux pastry for Orange-Blossom Éclairs (see page 184), enriched doughs (sweet rolls), flatbreads and light-as-air sponge cakes, such as the Iced Fancies (see page 186)

Learning new skills from different countries is what excites me more than anything else. Searing and finely slicing meats, as in the Asian Beef Carpaccio with Micro Herbs (see page 46), can be applied to many different meats and fish, and the method of making a semifreddo, for example, can be changed according to the season. I have added a twist to the Lemon-Meringue Cupcakes (see page 191) by replacing the buttercream topping with meringue, while in the Mayan Chocolate Cupcakes (see page 192) I've added a wake-up call to the tastebuds with chili and pink peppercorns, to make a cupcake with a surprising sting in its tail.

Another currently popular type of food that has caught my attention is ethnic street food, as well as wraps and sandwiches. These dishes are really the ones that create cravings, and I love serving a selection when

I have friends over. I have devised some fantastic examples of food to be eaten on the go: the Chicken Tikka Chapatis (see page 32), Lobster Rolls with Pea Shoots (see page 66), Vietnamese Beef Spring Rolls (see page 45), Cauliflower & Onion Pakoras with Mango & Fenugreek Salsa (see page 70) and Chorizo, Sweet Potato & Cilantro Quesadillas (see page 44) are just some examples. Use these recipes as starting points for your own innovative food-on-the-go.

HEALTHY FOOD

This is my fourth cookbook and it is the first book I have written where the emphasis is not on healthy eating and diet food. This doesn't mean that I don't always try to keep an overriding sense of freshness and cleanness to my food, and although these aren't diet recipes they are still pretty health-conscious. Eating well is not about starving yourself. My biggest piece of advice to anyone is make as much of your food from scratch as possible, because cooking your own food is the fastest route to a better diet.

This even applies to desserts: making a humdinger of a cake or pudding from scratch will not only enable you to realize how much fat and sugar goes into these dishes, but it will also make for a more satisfying meal. Purchased "goodies" are simply full of hidden nasties. I find my Rich Flourless Chocolate Cake (see page 190) unbelievably satisfying, even with just a small slice.

All the recipes in this book focus on using good ingredients and fresh new ways to prepare them as purely as possible, with Pan-Grilled Shrimp with Mango (see page 129) and Pea Shoot & Watercress Soup (see page 22) as good examples.

At a very simplistic level, color can be a good indicator of how healthy a plate of food is. Have you ever noticed how beige and bland-looking junk food can often be? If you bring in lots of veggies, herbs and spices, they add a burst of flavor on the palate and a color to the plate. Look at the Superfood Salad with Avocado & Lemon Dressings on page 68—it's a rainbow salad and full of so many top, nutrient-rich ingredients—or Saffron-Poached Chicken with Parsley & Tarragon Gremolata (see page 84). They really boost your spirits as well as your health.

I have always looked at food as more than just fuel. I am a great believer that the ingredients we consume make a huge difference to our minds and bodies. This is why these recipes include ingredients like salmon, sardines and tuna for their omega-3 oils and chicken, turkey and venison for their low-fat protein.

That is not to say that we shouldn't indulge sometimes, because life is too short not to love good food. This cookbook is not focused on diet, but it is focused on good ingredients and great cooking methods.

I find now that the methods of cooking I use most often tend to be lighter and healthier. I very rarely make creamy, heavy sauces or gravies, preferring herb-spiked dressings, as in Marinated Hanger Steak with Sweet Potato Mash & Cilantro-Honey Dressing (see page 106) or Roast Chicken with Salsa Verde (see page 88), and will often replace the traditional carbohydrates with vegetables. Also, taking inspiration from Asia means I use all those vibrant, immune-system-boosting ingredients like ginger, chili and garlic, plus the Asian cooking styles, which are often low in fat.

DIVE IN AND ENJOY!

I have divided the book into chapters containing light meals, main meals, desserts and baking. The light section really indicates light meals, appetizers or dishes you can mix and match and serve up a few at a time. The main meals are more substantial, but to be honest they are all quite interchangeable and I like the idea of mezze: eating lots of different flavors in one meal.

With new ingredients to discover across the world, and many old or even ancient ones that have been rediscovered to try, plus new combinations, new cooking methods and just new ways of looking at food, now is an exciting time to be cooking. Forget the rigid rules and elitism of yesteryear, and be prepared to embrace a modern take, with new flavor combinations and different ingredients.

I have loved writing these recipes and all the experimenting that went into them. I hope you will enjoy making them and eating them, and I also hope that some will become your favorites. Ultimately, I want you, too, to "Love Good Food."

Sophie Michell x

Light Meals

Pea Shoot & Watercress Soup

PREPARATION TIME: 15 minutes | COOKING TIME: 25 minutes | SERVES: 4

1 tablespoon olive oil
1 onion, finely chopped
2 leeks, trimmed and
  finely sliced
5 cups vegetable stock
7 ounces pea shoots,
  roughly chopped
1½ cups watercress,
  roughly chopped
freshly grated nutmeg,
  to taste
kosher salt and freshly
  ground black pepper

This is my healthy detox soup for the times when I want something comforting but packed full of goodness. The watercress gives it a lovely peppery flavor and the pea shoots add even more iron as well as antioxidants.

Heat the oil in a large saucepan over medium-low heat. Add the onion and leeks, cover and cook gently until softened and translucent, about 8 minutes; stir frequently and be careful not to let the onion and leek burn, as this will ruin the flavor. Pour in the stock and bring to a boil, then reduce the heat to low and simmer for 10 minutes.

Add the pea shoots and watercress and cook for 5 minutes longer. Remove from the heat. Using a handheld blender (or transferring the mixture to a blender or food processor), blitz until smooth. Reheat the soup until hot and season with nutmeg, salt and pepper.

Spring Minestrone

PREPARATION TIME: 20 minutes | COOKING TIME: 30 minutes | SERVES: 4

1 tablespoon olive oil
4 ounces pancetta, diced
1 onion, finely chopped
2 garlic cloves, minced
3 celery sticks, finely
  diced
1 leek, finely diced
1 zucchini, diced
½ cup green beans, cut
  into 1-inch pieces
4 cups vegetable stock
a large pinch of oregano
1 cup broccoli florets
¾ cup asparagus tips
kosher salt and freshly
  ground black pepper

TO SERVE
1 small handful of
  micro basil leaves
1 small handful of
  Parmesan cheese
  shavings

Minestrone is a classic and very versatile vegetable soup. I add more root veggies and legumes during winter and more tomatoes during summer, making it the ultimate seasonal soup. This recipe is a rarefied version, using some lovely delicate spring vegetables.

Heat the oil in a large saucepan over medium-high heat. Add the pancetta and cook, stirring frequently, for 5 minutes. Reduce the heat to medium-low and add the onion, garlic, celery and leek. Cook until the onion is softened and translucent, about 10 minutes.

Add the zucchini and green beans and cook for 5 minutes longer, then add the stock and oregano and bring to a boil. Reduce the heat to low and simmer gently for 5 minutes. Add the broccoli and asparagus and simmer for another 5 minutes.

Remove from the heat and season with salt and pepper. Serve immediately, sprinkled with a little micro basil and with Parmesan shavings scattered over.

Herb Consommé

PREPARATION TIME: 25 minutes | COOKING TIME: 20 minutes | SERVES: 4

1 boneless, skinless
  chicken breast half
1 small handful of parsley
1 small handful of
  tarragon
1 garlic clove, peeled
1 leek, roughly chopped
2 carrots, peeled and
  roughly chopped
1 celery stick, roughly
  chopped
1 small onion, roughly
  diced
4 cups chicken stock
4 egg whites, lightly
  whisked
kosher salt and freshly
  ground black pepper

TO SERVE
1 tablespoon finely
  chopped chives
1 small handful of
  micro tarragon
1 small handful of
  micro basil
1 small handful of
  micro mint

To be able to clarify a stock is a classic skill. I have included the technique in this book because a clear, golden, flavorsome stock is an item of beauty, and with the addition of micro herbs it makes a delicate prelude to any meal.

Put the chicken breast, parsley, tarragon, garlic and all the vegetables in a blender or food processor and blitz until finely chopped.

Pour the stock into a large saucepan and heat over medium-high heat. When the stock is hot, stir in the egg whites and the chicken and vegetable mix. Bring to a boil, stirring continuously to prevent the egg whites from sinking to the bottom of the pan or sticking to the sides.

As soon as the stock begins to boil, stop stirring and reduce the heat to medium-low. Simmer, uncovered, for 15 minutes, then remove from the heat. A layer of chicken and egg white will form a "lid" on the surface of the liquid. When it does, make a small hole in the center to let out the steam.

Using a ladle, carefully scoop out the clear liquid and pass it through a fine strainer, ideally lined with cheesecloth, into a clean pan. Season with salt and pepper and very gently reheat until almost boiling.

Mix the chives and micro herbs together and sprinkle some over each bowl of soup before serving.

Butternut Squash, Chili & Maple Syrup Soup

PREPARATION TIME: 15 minutes | COOKING TIME: 45 minutes | SERVES: 4

1 tablespoon olive oil
1 onion, roughly chopped
2 garlic cloves, finely
    chopped
1 teaspoon dried chili
    flakes
1 rosemary sprig
4 cups peeled and seeded
    butternut squash, cut
    into cubes (about
    1 pound 2 ounces)
4 cups vegetable stock
1 teaspoon maple syrup
kosher salt and freshly
    ground black pepper

TO SERVE
crème fraîche

This soup is a smooth, unassuming and quietly comforting bowl. I like to add a little chili and rosemary for a savory note, and maple syrup for sweet caramel undertones. It's very easy to make.

Heat the oil in a large saucepan over medium-low heat. Add the onion and garlic and cook gently, covered so the juices sweat out, until softened and translucent, about 8 minutes; stir frequently and be careful that the onion and garlic don't burn. Add the chili flakes, rosemary leaves and butternut squash. Replace the lid and continue to cook for 5 minutes longer.

Pour in the stock and bring to a boil. Reduce the heat to low and simmer, covered, until the squash is soft, about 30 minutes.

Remove the saucepan from the heat and take out the rosemary sprig. Add the maple syrup and season with salt and pepper. Using a handheld blender (or transferring the mixture to a blender or food processor), blitz until very smooth. Reheat the soup until hot, then serve with a generous spoonful of crème fraîche swirled into each bowl.

Jerusalem Artichoke Soup with Sourdough-Parmesan Croûtons

PREPARATION TIME: 25 minutes | COOKING TIME: 40 minutes | SERVES: 4

11 ounces Jerusalem
   artichokes
squeeze of lemon juice
1½ teaspoons olive oil
1 onion, finely chopped
4 cups vegetable stock
scant ½ cup heavy cream
kosher salt and freshly
   ground black pepper

CROÛTONS
3 slices of sourdough
   bread
1 tablespoon olive oil
¼ cup grated Parmesan
   cheese

Jerusalem artichokes have a nutty flavor, quite similar to globe artichokes. They look very uninviting when raw, but produce a wonderfully smooth soup. The sourdough croûtons are chewy, crispy and cheesy, all in one bite.

To prepare the Jerusalem artichokes, first fill a large bowl with cold water and add a big squeeze of lemon juice. Peel the artichokes with a small knife or swivel-bladed vegetable peeler, then slice them thinly and immediately put the slices into the prepared water. This will prevent the artichokes from oxidizing and turning black, which happens very quickly.

Heat the oil in a large saucepan over medium-low heat. Add the onion and cook gently, covered so the juices sweat out, until softened and translucent, about 8 minutes; stir frequently and be careful the onion doesn't burn. Pour in the stock. Drain the artichokes and add to the pan, then bring to a boil. Reduce the heat to low and simmer, covered, for 30 minutes.

Meanwhile, to make the croûtons, heat the broiler. Cut the crusts off the sourdough and discard, then cut the bread into cubes. Put the bread cubes on a baking sheet, drizzle the oil over and sprinkle the Parmesan evenly over the cubes. Put the sheet under the broiler, about 4 inches from the heat, and toast, tossing occasionally, until golden and crisp, about 10 minutes. Let cool.

Remove the soup from the heat. Using a handheld blender (or transferring the soup to a food processor or blender), blitz until very smooth. Add the cream and season with salt and pepper. Reheat the soup until hot, then serve topped with the croûtons.

Pan-Grilled Chicken, Beet, Manchego & Candied Pecan Salad

PREPARATION TIME: 15 minutes | COOKING TIME: 30 minutes | SERVES: 4

8 small raw beets, scrubbed
1 tablespoon olive oil
4 boneless, skinless chicken breast halves
2 tablespoons butter
scant 1 cup pecan halves
1/4 cup packed light brown sugar
1 large head of Belgian endive, trimmed and broken into leaves
2 heads of radicchio, trimmed and broken into leaves
4 ounces Manchego cheese shavings
kosher salt and freshly ground black pepper

DRESSING
1 teaspoon Dijon mustard
1 tablespoon white wine vinegar
3 tablespoons olive oil
2 teaspoons walnut oil

I love serving this modern bistro-style salad for a light lunch. The deep pink beets, bitter endive and sweet crunchy nuts form a perfectly balanced dish and the colors are beautiful.

Preheat the oven to 400°F. Put the beets in a baking pan, drizzle the oil over and season with salt and pepper. Cover the pan with foil, then roast until cooked through, about 30 minutes. Remove from the oven and set aside until cool enough to handle. Wearing rubber gloves to prevent your hands and nails from turning pink, slide the skins off the beets and cut the beets into quarters.

Heat a ridged grill pan over medium-high heat, then cook the chicken breasts until golden brown and cooked through, about 6 minutes per side. To test if they are done, insert the tip of a sharp knife into the thickest part of the breast—the juices should run clear. Put the breasts on a plate, cover with foil and let rest.

Melt the butter in a frying pan over medium heat until it begins to foam. Add the pecans and cook for 3 minutes, turning occasionally, then add the brown and granulated sugars and cook until the nuts are golden and caramelized, about 3 more minutes. Remove from the heat and let cool slightly.

To make the dressing, whisk all the ingredients together in a small bowl until thoroughly combined. Put the endive, radicchio and beets into a large bowl and toss together, then toss with the dressing. Divide among the plates.

Cut each of the chicken breasts on the diagonal into three to five slices and arrange on the beets and leaves. Scatter the Manchego shavings and candied pecans over the salad and serve.

Chicken Tikka Chapatis

PREPARATION TIME: 15 minutes plus 2 hours marinating time | COOKING TIME: 10 minutes | SERVES: 4

2 boneless, skinless chicken breast halves, cut into strips
1 heaped tablespoon tikka paste
1 tablespoon plain yogurt
2–3 tablespoons mango chutney
4 wholewheat chapatis
kosher salt and freshly ground pepper

HERB & CHICKPEA YOGURT
2 heaped tablespoons roughly chopped mint leaves
2 heaped tablespoons roughly chopped cilantro leaves
1/2 teaspoon cumin seeds
2/3 cup plain yogurt
scant 1 cup drained, canned chickpeas

These grab-and-go wonders are fab for packed lunches and quick bites. I kid you not: everyone loves these wraps and they get gobbled up within minutes.

Put the chicken in a large bowl and toss with the tikka paste and yogurt until the chicken is well coated. Cover with plastic wrap and let marinate in the refrigerator for 2 hours (or longer if this is more convenient).

Meanwhile, make the yogurt dip. Mix together the mint, cilantro, cumin seeds and yogurt in a large bowl until thoroughly combined. Cover with plastic wrap and refrigerate until required.

When you are ready to eat, heat the broiler. Put the chicken strips on a baking sheet, season with salt and pepper and broil, 3–4 inches from the heat, turning occasionally, until cooked through, about 10 minutes. Meanwhile, add the chickpeas to the yogurt dip and mix until thoroughly combined.

Spread a thick layer of mango chutney on top of the chapatis, then top with the herb and chickpea yogurt. Divide the broiled chicken among the chapatis, then roll up and serve.

Warm Duck & Lychee Salad

PREPARATION TIME: 20 minutes | COOKING TIME: 2 hours | SERVES: 4

4 duck legs
2-inch piece of fresh
   gingerroot, peeled and
   finely chopped
1 cup drained
   canned lychees
4 scallions, finely sliced
½ head of napa cabbage,
   thickly sliced
kosher salt and freshly
   ground black pepper

DRESSING
1 teaspoon sesame seeds
1 hot red chili, finely diced
2 teaspoons soy sauce
½ teaspoon toasted
   sesame oil
1 teaspoon Chinese rice
   wine vinegar

Slow-roasted duck legs are great for making a fairly cheap but very tasty salad; I love the contrast between the sweet lychees and the savory duck. With the addition of herbs and chili, it really is a great salad to have for lunch or as part of a big Asian feast.

Preheat the oven to 320°F. Season the duck legs generously with salt, then put them in a deep roasting pan and scatter the ginger over them. Cover the pan with foil and roast for 1½ hours. Turn the oven temperature up to 400°F, remove the foil and roast until the duck is browned and the meat easily pulls away from the bone, about 30 minutes longer. Remove the duck from the oven and let cool slightly.

Using two forks, shred the duck meat into small pieces and put in a bowl. Mix in a little of the duck fat, for flavor, plus the ginger, and season with salt and pepper. Let cool a little more, then add the lychees, scallions and napa cabbage and toss until well combined.

Whisk together all the dressing ingredients in a small bowl, then pour over the duck and lychee salad and toss until all the ingredients are well coated. Serve immediately.

Pea-Shoot Pancakes with Crispy Pancetta & Sweet Chili Sauce

PREPARATION TIME: 20 minutes | **COOKING TIME:** 20 minutes | **MAKES:** 8 (2 per serving)

2 ounces pea shoots, plus extra for scattering
$1/3$ cup heavy cream
1 egg
$1/2$ cup self-rising flour
$1/2$ teaspoon sugar
1 cup frozen peas, thawed and roughly crushed
8 slices of pancetta or bacon, cut into fine strips
3–4 tablespoons butter
3 heaped tablespoons sweet chili sauce or chili jam
kosher salt and freshly ground black pepper

TO SERVE
$1/2$ cup crème fraîche

These small, bright green pancakes are a real showstopper. I also make them bite-sized for canapés, and sometimes top them with smoked salmon and chives instead of the pancetta and chili sauce.

Put the pea shoots in a blender or food processor and blitz until finely chopped. Add the cream, egg, flour and sugar, then blitz again to form a smooth batter. Season with salt and pepper and fold in the peas.

Heat the broiler and spread out the pancetta on a baking sheet. Broil the pancetta slices until crisp, about 4 minutes per side. Cover with foil to keep warm and set aside.

Heat a large frying pan over medium heat, then melt 2 tablespoons of the butter in the pan. Using a heaped tablespoon of batter for each pancake, cook four at a time until golden brown, about 3 minutes per side. Remove the pancakes to a plate lined with paper towels. Cover with a kitchen towel to keep warm while you cook the remaining pancakes, adding more butter to the pan as required.

Serve the pancakes with the pancetta on top and chili sauce drizzled over. Add a dollop of crème fraîche and a garnish of pea shoots.

Ham Hock Terrine with Mustard Fruits

PREPARATION TIME: 25 minutes, plus overnight setting time | COOKING TIME: 2½ hours | SERVES: 10

2 fresh ham hocks, about
  5½ pounds in total
1 onion, quartered
2 carrots, peeled and
  roughly chopped
2 celery sticks, roughly
  chopped
1 bouquet garni
4 black peppercorns
2 teaspoons white wine
  vinegar
2 shallots, roughly
  chopped
1 large bunch of parsley,
  finely chopped
2 gelatin sheets
4 ounces mustard fruits
  in their syrup
kosher salt and freshly
  ground black pepper

TO SERVE
2½ cups small arugula
  leaves
toasted sourdough or
  rustic white bread

Ham hocks are cheap and full of flavor. They take some cooking but make great terrines, salads and soups. I like to serve this terrine with *mostarda di frutta* (mustard fruits).

Put the ham hocks, onion, carrots, celery, bouquet garni and peppercorns in a large pot and cover with water. Bring to a boil, then reduce the heat to low and simmer until the meat is falling off the bone, about 2 hours. Set aside until the meat is cool enough to handle, then remove it from the bones and shred into smaller pieces. Cover with plastic wrap and leave to one side.

With a slotted spoon, remove the vegetables and any remaining bones from the pot, then simmer the stock over low heat until it has reduced to about 1¾ cups, about 30 minutes. Don't let the stock bubble too much or it will turn cloudy. Stir in the vinegar, shallots and parsley. Taste and add salt and pepper, if needed.

Cover the sides and bottom of a large terrine mold or loaf pan with two layers of plastic wrap, leaving plenty of extra wrap hanging over the sides. Put the gelatin sheets in a small bowl of cold water and soak until softened, about 5 minutes, then squeeze to remove any excess water and stir into the stock until completely melted.

Press the shredded meat into the prepared mold and pour the stock over. Cover with the overhanging plastic wrap and refrigerate for 30 minutes to set. Cut a piece of cardboard to fit snugly on top of the terrine, then weight the cardboard down on top of the terrine with cans of food or something else that is heavy, and return it to the refrigerate to set overnight. Slice the terrine and serve with the mustard fruits, arugula leaves and toasted bread.

"These jewel-like mustard fruits add color and piquancy to any dish."

Fava Bean, Pea Shoot & Prosciutto Salad with Truffle Dressing

PREPARATION TIME: 15 minutes, plus 15 minutes thawing time | SERVES: 4

1 cup frozen fava or baby
   lima beans, thawed
1 cup frozen peas, thawed
2 heads of baby romaine,
   trimmed and broken
   into leaves
12 slices of prosciutto
kosher salt and freshly
   ground black pepper

TRUFFLE DRESSING
1 teaspoon Dijon mustard
4 teaspoons white wine
   vinegar
3½ tablespoons olive oil
a splash of truffle oil
1 teaspoon chopped
   truffle paste (optional)

TO SERVE
1 ounce pea shoots
scant 1 ounce Parmesan
   cheese shavings

This salad is brought into the realms of gourmet food with the addition of the truffle-oil dressing. Fava beans are great when popped out of their little casings, and the prosciutto with Parmesan shavings finish the dish perfectly.

To make the dressing, whisk all the ingredients together in a small bowl until thoroughly combined. Set aside to let the flavors develop.

Pop the thawed fava beans out of their pale outer skins and mix with the peas in a large bowl. Add the lettuce, then drizzle the dressing over and mix well. Season with salt and pepper.

Divide the lettuce leaves and the pea and bean mixture among four serving plates. Arrange the prosciutto on the salad, scatter the pea shoots and Parmesan shavings on top and serve.

Feta, Sun-Dried Tomato & Pancetta Mini Frittatas

PREPARATION TIME: 15 minutes | COOKING TIME: 15 minutes | MAKES: 4

olive oil, for greasing
8 slices of pancetta
7 ounces feta cheese,
   crumbled
1/2 cup basil leaves, torn
12 sun-dried tomato
   halves in oil, drained
10 eggs
scant 1/2 cup milk
kosher salt and freshly
   ground black pepper

Frittatas are great: they are quick and easy to make and you can be quite creative with them. Try different cheeses, herbs and meats to vary the flavors. Children love these protein-packed bites for snacks and in lunchboxes.

Preheat the oven to 400°F. Grease four ramekins and line them with the pancetta. Set them in a shallow baking pan.

Put an equal quantity of the feta into each of the ramekins. Divide the basil leaves among the ramekins and put three sun-dried tomato halves, cut-side up, on top of the basil.

Whisk the eggs and milk together in a large measure or pitcher and season with salt and pepper. Pour into the ramekins.

Bake until the frittatas are just set and starting to brown, about 15 minutes. Remove from the oven and let cool in the ramekins, then remove and serve warm or cold.

Note: If you would rather make six smaller frittatas, use a 6-cup muffin pan and divide the ingredients equally among the cups.

Spiced Lamb Flatbreads

PREPARATION TIME: 40 minutes, plus making the dough | COOKING TIME: 30 minutes | SERVES: 4

1 tablespoon olive oil

1 onion, finely chopped

2 garlic cloves, minced

14 ounces ground lamb (scant 2 cups)

½ teaspoon ground cinnamon

½ teaspoon ground allspice

a pinch of ground cumin

a pinch of ground coriander

1 tablespoon tomato paste

1 tablespoon pomegranate molasses, plus extra for drizzling (optional)

1 recipe quantity Flatbreads dough (see page 202)

flour, for dusting

3 tablespoons pine nuts

1 small handful of micro mint leaves

the seeds tapped out of 1 pomegranate

kosher salt and freshly ground black pepper

When I lived in Beirut, I used to buy these flatbreads straight out of the oven from a hole-in-the-wall takeout place near my house. The food was fabulous there and I still miss it...

Heat the oil in a large saucepan over medium heat. Add the onion, garlic and lamb and stir until well combined. Cover the pan with a tight-fitting lid and cook, stirring occasionally, until the ingredients start to turn golden and come together, about 10 minutes. Add the spices and tomato paste and season with salt and pepper. Stir in the pomegranate molasses, then remove the pan from the heat.

Preheat the oven to 350°F. Take the flatbread dough from the refrigerator and turn out onto a lightly floured surface. Roll the dough into a ball, then divide into eight pieces (for medium-size flatbreads) or 24 pieces (for bite-size flatbreads). Roll each piece into a circle and flatten it with the heel of your hand, then roll into a thin disk with a rolling pin. Put the disks on a baking sheet and spread the lamb mixture over the top. Bake until crisp and golden, about 15 minutes.

Remove from the oven and top with the pine nuts, micro mint and pomegranate seeds. Drizzle a little more pomegranate molasses over the flatbreads before serving, if desired.

Chorizo, Sweet Potato & Cilantro Quesadillas

PREPARATION TIME: 20 minutes | COOKING TIME: 1 hour 35 minutes | SERVES: 6

7 ounces sweet potatoes
5½ ounces uncooked (Spanish) chorizo
1 red onion, roughly chopped
1 hot red chili, seeded and finely chopped
4 ounces feta cheese
1 small handful of cilantro leaves, plus extra for serving
6 flour tortillas

TO SERVE
3½ ounces pickled jalapeños
scant ½ cup sour cream
1 lime, cut into wedges

Quesadillas are wonderful to make for last-minute nibbles as they are so versatile. You can stuff them with all sorts of fillings, including the spicy and delicious combination I have used here.

Put the sweet potatoes in a saucepan of boiling water, reduce the heat to low and simmer, covered, until cooked through, about 20 minutes. Be very careful not to overcook. Drain the sweet potatoes in a colander and let cool, then cut into small dice.

Heat a frying pan over medium-high heat. Crumble in the chorizo and cook, stirring frequently, until the oil is released, about 4 minutes. Add the onion and chili and cook, stirring occasionally, until browned, about 8 minutes. Add the diced sweet potato, feta and cilantro and toss well. Remove from the heat.

Preheat the oven to 320°F. Put three baking sheets or pans in the oven to heat. Lay one tortilla flat on a cutting board. Spread one-sixth of the chorizo and potato mixture over half of the tortilla, then fold over the other half to make a half-moon. Repeat with the remaining tortillas and chorizo and potato mixture.

Heat a large frying pan or ridged grill pan over medium heat. Lay a quesadilla in the pan and cook until crisp and golden, about 5 minutes per side. Remove from the pan and put on one of the baking sheets in the oven to keep warm while you cook the remaining quesadillas, adding them in turn to the baking sheets to keep warm.

Cut the quesadillas in half, put them on a platter and sprinkle some extra cilantro over them. Serve immediately with the pickled jalapeños, sour cream and lime wedges.

Vietnamese Beef Spring Rolls

PREPARATION TIME: 25 minutes, plus 1 hour marinating time and making the sauce | COOKING TIME: 8 minutes | SERVES: 4

1 boneless steak,
  preferably sirloin,
  about 11 ounces
3½ ounces rice vermicelli
a drizzle of toasted
  sesame oil
1 small handful of micro
  mint leaves or roughly
  chopped mint leaves
1 small handful of
  micro cilantro leaves
  or roughly chopped
  cilantro leaves
8 rice-paper skins
½ hothouse cucumber,
  cut into matchsticks
1 carrot, peeled and cut
  into matchsticks
kosher salt and freshly
  ground black pepper

MARINADE
2 garlic cloves, finely
  chopped
1 lemongrass stalk, outer
  leaves removed, end cut
  off and bruised
grated zest of 1 lime
1 hot chili, finely chopped
1 teaspoon brown sugar
1 tablespoon dry sherry

TO SERVE
Dipping Sauce
  (see page 198)

These light and fresh spring rolls are so much better than the deep-fried version. Use big shrimp or cooked chicken strips for a change if you don't feel like beef.

To make the marinade, mix all the ingredients together in a large bowl. Add the steak and spoon the marinade over it. Cover with plastic wrap and let marinate in the refrigerator for 1 hour.

Put the noodles into a bowl and cover with boiling water. Let soak for 5 minutes, then drain in a colander and refresh under cold water. Return the noodles to the bowl and toss with the sesame oil.

Heat a frying pan over medium-high heat. Pat the steak dry with paper towels and season with salt and pepper, then put it in the hot pan and sear until well browned but still pink and juicy inside, about 4 minutes per side. Remove from the heat and let rest on a plate for 5 minutes, then cut into thin slices. Meanwhile, stir the micro mint and micro cilantro into the dipping sauce, reserving a large pinch of each for garnishing the spring rolls.

Pour some hot water into a deep saucer or soup bowl. Taking one rice-paper skin at a time, soak the sheet in the water until softened. Remove, shake off any excess water and lay flat on a cutting board. Leaving a ½-inch border clear at each end, arrange horizontally along the middle of the rice paper: a big pinch each of the noodles, cucumber and carrot and a few slices of beef. Fold over the ends, then roll up tightly. Put on a plate and cover with a kitchen towel. Continue making up the remaining spring rolls. Serve sprinkled with the reserved micro herbs, with the dipping sauce on the side.

Asian Beef Carpaccio with Micro Herbs

PREPARATION TIME: 15 minutes, plus minimum 30 minutes chilling time | COOKING TIME: 15 minutes | SERVES: 4

1 beef tenderloin roast, about 14 ounces
2/3 cup vegetable oil
8 garlic cloves, finely sliced lengthwise
1 small handful of micro cilantro
1 small handful of micro Thai purple basil
kosher salt and freshly ground pepper

DRESSING
2 tablespoons soy sauce
1/2 teaspoon sugar
1 hot red chili, seeded and finely chopped
1/2 teaspoon toasted sesame oil

This is my version of a carpaccio: slightly rustic and lightly seared on the outside, with crunchy garlic chips and a sweet, salty and lightly spiced dressing. The garlic chips are brilliant and the flavors work well, especially the unique aniseed tones of the Thai purple basil.

Heat a nonstick frying pan over high heat until smoking hot. Season the beef well with salt and pepper, then put it in the pan and sear, turning, until a brown crust forms all over, 8–10 minutes. Remove from the pan and let cool.

When the beef has cooled (it doesn't need to be cold), roll it several times in plastic wrap as tightly as possible to create a sausage shape. Tie at both ends and refrigerate for 30 minutes to 1 hour. Meanwhile, whisk all the dressing ingredients together in a small bowl until thoroughly combined.

Heat the vegetable oil in a small, heavy-based saucepan over medium heat until hot. Test by dropping in a slice of garlic, which should sizzle immediately. Add the garlic slices in batches, so they have plenty of space around them, and fry until light golden brown. (Keep an eye on the garlic, because it will cook quickly and can burn easily.) Using a slotted spoon, remove from the oil and drain on paper towels.

When you are ready to eat, remove the beef from the refrigerator and slice it very thinly. Serve overlapping slices sprinkled with the micro cilantro, micro Thai purple basil and garlic chips and with the dressing drizzled over.

Sesame Tuna with Wasabi Potato Salad & Pink Grapefruit Dressing

PREPARATION TIME: 20 minutes, plus making the mayonnaise | COOKING TIME: 25 minutes | SERVES: 4

1 tablespoon sesame seeds
4 thick tuna steaks, about 6 ounces each
14 ounces boiling potatoes
1 tablespoon Mayonnaise (see page 199)
1 teaspoon wasabi paste
1 pink grapefruit
1 tablespoon light soy sauce
1 teaspoon toasted sesame oil
1 teaspoon peanut oil, plus extra for frying
2 ounces mizuna, plus extra for scattering
1 tablespoon micro shiso cress, plus extra for scattering

When I started developing this recipe I wasn't sure whether it would come out as I was hoping. In fact it did—and the seared pink tuna, hot creamy wasabi and pink grapefuit are excellent together. It's a fusion dish I suppose, especially if you can find Japanese mayonnaise.

Sprinkle the sesame seeds onto a plate and press both sides of each tuna steak into them. Move the steaks to a clean plate, cover with plastic wrap and refrigerate.

Put the potatoes in a large saucepan, cover with water and bring to a boil. Turn the heat down and simmer, covered, until cooked through, about 15 minutes. Drain the potatoes in a colander and let cool.

Mix the mayonnaise and wasabi together in a large bowl. Rub the skins off the potatoes and cut the flesh into small cubes. Add the potatoes to the mayonnaise and toss until well coated. Set aside.

Using a sharp knife, peel the grapefruit, removing all the skin and pith, then carefully cut into sections, working over a bowl so any juice is caught. Add the soy sauce and the sesame and peanut oils to the bowl and mix with the juices and grapefruit sections. Add the mizuna and micro cress and toss again.

Heat a splash of peanut oil in a large frying pan over medium heat. Add the tuna and sear until lightly browned but still pink inside, about 4 minutes per side. Serve the seared tuna with the wasabi potato salad and the pink grapefruit dressing, garnished with extra mizuna and micro cress.

Sardines Wrapped in Grape Leaves with Verjuice-Poached Grapes

PREPARATION TIME: 20 minutes | COOKING TIME: 30 minutes | SERVES: 4

8 bottled grape leaves
8 plump sardines, gutted and heads removed

POACHED GRAPES
3 tablespoons verjuice or white wine
2 teaspoons sugar
11 ounces white or green seedless grapes (about 1½ cups)

HERB CROSTINI
8 small slices of rustic French bread, cut on the diagonal
1 tablespoon finely chopped flat-leaf parsley
1 teaspoon finely chopped tarragon
3 tablespoons extra-virgin olive oil
1 teaspoon grated lemon zest
kosher salt

I love cooking sardines wrapped in grape leaves, because they keep in more of the moisture and add flavor. I have added a slightly sour aspect with the verjuice-poached grapes, and chosen some herb crostini for some crunch.

To make the poached grapes, put the verjuice, sugar and ¾ cup water into a saucepan, bring to a boil and simmer for 10 minutes. Add the grapes to the pan and simmer for 10 minutes longer, then remove from the heat.

To make the herb crostini, heat the broiler, then toast the slices of bread on each side until crisp. Mix together the parsley, tarragon, olive oil and lemon zest in a small dish, then season with salt. Spread a little on each slice of bread.

Wrap a grape leaf around each sardine. Fry in a large frying pan over medium heat until just cooked through, 4 to 6 minutes per side. Serve the sardines with the grapes and herb crostini.

"The verjuice-poached grapes balance the oiliness of the sardines perfectly."

Sea Bass Sashimi with Pomegranate & Micro Herbs

PREPARATION TIME: 20 minutes | SERVES: 4

4 very fresh, skin-on sea
  bass fillets, about
  7 ounces total weight
the seeds tapped out of
  1 pomegranate
1 small handful of mixed
  micro herbs
1 small handful of radish
  sprouts
kosher salt and freshly
  ground black pepper

LEMON DRESSING
juice of 1 lemon
3 tablespoons extra-
  virgin olive oil

You need super-fresh fish for this Beirut Beach Club-inspired dish, and the sourness of the pomegranate really works well with it. It's a very quick dish, designed to be eaten immediately.

Lay the sea bass, skin-side down, on a cutting board. The board needs to be secure, so put it on a dampened kitchen towel, if necessary. Using a sharp knife, carefully cut off thin slices of fish on a diagonal. Lay the slices on a separate cutting board or plate, cover with plastic wrap and refrigerate while you make the dressing.

Mix the lemon dressing ingredients together in a small bowl and season with salt and pepper.

Arrange the sea bass slices on each plate in a decorative way. Sprinkle with the pomegranate seeds and drizzle the lemon dressing over, then arrange the micro herbs and radish sprouts in the middle. Serve immediately.

Shrimp Ceviche

PREPARATION TIME: 15 minutes, plus 1 hour marinating time | COOKING TIME: 10 minutes | SERVES: 4

14 ounces peeled, cooked tiger shrimp or large shrimp
4 ounces cherry tomatoes, quartered
1 red onion, finely chopped
1 red bell pepper, seeded and finely diced
1 tablespoon minced pickled jalapeño
1 heaped tablespoon roughly chopped cilantro leaves
juice of 1 lime
juice of ½ lemon
2 ears of corn, shucked and kernels sliced off the cob

TO SERVE
4 ounces tortilla or corn chips

Ceviche is traditionally fresh raw fish marinated in citrus juice. My version is a twist on this to make a modern type of shrimp cocktail. You can serve it in little glass dishes and use the chips to scoop up the juicy shrimp, with blue corn chips looking especially stunning.

Slice the shrimp in half down the middle and devein, then put in a large bowl. Add the cherry tomatoes, onion, red pepper, jalapeño, cilantro and the lime and lemon juices, and toss until well combined.

Heat the broiler. Spread the corn kernels in a small baking pan and broil, quite close to the heat, until they are slightly charred, about 10 minutes, stirring occasionally. Let the corn cool, then stir into the shrimp and vegetable mixture. Cover the bowl with plastic wrap and let marinate in the refrigerator for 1 hour. Serve with tortilla chips.

Shrimp & Samphire Tarts

PREPARATION TIME: 30 minutes, plus 30 minutes resting time | COOKING TIME: 50 minutes | MAKES: 4

1 cup + 2 tablespoons (2 sticks + 2 tablespoons) butter, chilled and roughly diced

3½ cups all-purpose flour, plus extra for dusting

1 teaspoon olive oil

2 large shallots, finely diced

2 eggs

3 tablespoons heavy cream

¼ teaspoon ground mace

7 ounces peeled, cooked very small shrimp

4 ounces samphire or fine asparagus spears

kosher salt and freshly ground black pepper

TO SERVE
mixed salad greens

Blitz the butter and flour in a blender or food processor until they resemble fine breadcrumbs. With the motor running, gradually add 3–4 tablespoons ice-cold water until you get a smooth dough—you don't want it to be too wet. Turn the dough out onto a lightly floured surface and shape into a ball, then wrap in plastic wrap and refrigerate for 30 minutes.

Preheat the oven to 350°F. Roll out the dough on a lightly floured surface to ⅛ inch thick. Using a round pastry cutter about 5½ inches in diameter, or a saucer of similar size and a sharp knife, cut out four discs and use them to line four 3½-inch tart pans. (There will be some leftover pastry: wrap in plastic wrap and freeze for another day.) Line each pastry shell with parchment paper and weight the paper down with dried beans or rice. Bake for 15 minutes. Remove the weights and paper, prick the bottom of each pastry shell with a fork and bake until the pastry is just starting to turn golden, about 5 more minutes.

Meanwhile, heat the oil in a frying pan over medium-low heat. Add the shallots and fry gently until softened and translucent, about 5 minutes. Remove from the heat.

Whisk the eggs and cream together in a bowl until well combined. Add the mace and season with salt and pepper, then add the shallots and shrimp and stir well.

Put the tart pans on a baking sheet and carefully pour the egg and shrimp mixture into the pastry shells, making sure the shrimp are equally divided among them. Nestle the samphire into the filling. (If using asparagus, trim the spears as required to fit neatly.)

Bake until the filling is just set and golden, about 20 minutes. Remove from the oven and serve either hot or warm with mixed salad greens.

"This is a novel way to use shrimp. The samphire adds another layer of seaside flavors."

Beet-Cured Salmon Gravlax

PREPARATION TIME: 25 minutes, plus 24 hours curing time | SERVES: 4 (plus a little extra)

1 skin-on salmon fillet, about 1¾ pounds
scant 1 cup coarse sea salt
½ cup packed brown sugar
grated zest of 1 lemon
1 teaspoon freshly ground black pepper
7 ounces raw beets, peeled and grated (about 1½ cups)
1 small handful of tarragon leaves, roughly chopped
1 small handful of edible flowers, such as borage, pansy and chive blossoms, for scattering

DRESSING
1 tablespoon bottled horseradish
1 tablespoon wholegrain mustard
1 teaspoon white wine vinegar
2 teaspoons sugar
kosher salt and freshly ground black pepper

TO SERVE
blinis, rye bread or Oaty Soda Bread (see page 181), (optional)

This dish fulfills my love of pretty colors, delicate flavors and simple but impressive techniques. Curing salmon is one of those processes that sounds so much harder and more time-consuming than it actually is, and the result is really fantastic! The beets add amazing colorful edges.

Check the salmon for pin bones and remove, then trim off any excess fatty bits from the edges of the salmon.

Mix the salt, sugar, lemon zest and pepper together in a small bowl. Put the fish, skin-side down, on a plastic tray and pat the salt mixture on top in an even layer. Spread the grated beets over the salt mixture, then cover with plastic wrap and put a second tray or cutting board on top of the salmon. Put weights such as cans of food on the tray, then refrigerate to cure for at least 24 hours.

Whisk all the ingredients for the dressing together with 2 teaspoons water until thoroughly combined, then cover and refrigerate with the salmon.

Scrape the beet and salt mixture off the salmon and discard. Quickly rinse the salmon under cold water and pat dry with paper towels. Put the salmon on a cutting board and, using a very sharp knife, cut it on the diagonal into thin slices. Hold onto the skin while you cut to keep the fish steady, and discard it when you have finished cutting the fish.

Drizzle the dressing over the salmon, then scatter the tarragon and edible flowers over. Serve with blinis, rye bread or soda bread, if desired.

Hot & Sour Shrimp Salad

PREPARATION TIME: 20 minutes | COOKING TIME: 2 minutes | SERVES: 4

7 ounces snow peas
  (about 1½ cups)
1 cup bean sprouts
4 ounces pea shoots
2 carrots, peeled and cut
  into thin strips with a
  swivel-bladed peeler
14 ounces peeled, cooked
  tiger shrimp or large
  shrimp
1 small handful of
  cilantro leaves, roughly
  chopped, for sprinkling

HOT & SOUR DRESSING
1 tablespoon peanuts
1 hot red chili
a pinch of sugar
a pinch of hot chili
  powder or dried
  chili flakes
1 teaspoon fish sauce
1 teaspoon lime juice
1 teaspoon rice wine
  vinegar
1 teaspoon soy sauce

Thai and Southeast Asian cooking is all about balance of flavors. Sweet, salty, hot and sour: these all need to be combined in the perfect ratio. Test as you go along and adapt to your own tastes. You can serve this as an appetizer followed by Beef Rendang (see page 110) or Pad Thai (see page 128).

To make the hot and sour dressing, put the peanuts, chili and sugar in a small blender and grind to a smooth paste (or use a mortar and pestle). Scrape the paste into a small bowl and mix with the remaining dressing ingredients until well combined. Set aside.

Bring a saucepan of water to a boil. Add the snow peas and boil for 2 minutes, then drain and refresh under cold water to stop the cooking process. Drain well, then tip the snow peas into a large bowl and toss with the bean sprouts, pea shoots, carrots and shrimp. Pour the dressing over the salad and stir well.

This salad can be made up to 1 hour before serving with the cilantro sprinkled over the top.

Five-Spice Scallops with Fennel Purée & Orange Dressing

PREPARATION TIME: 20 minutes | COOKING TIME: 25 minutes | SERVES: 4

2 teaspoons Chinese
   five-spice powder
12 sea scallops
1 teaspoon olive oil
kosher salt and freshly
   ground black pepper
1 small handful of cress,
   for sprinkling

FENNEL PURÉE
2 bulbs of fennel,
   trimmed and roughly
   chopped
2 tablespoons butter
1¾ cups vegetable stock
1 tablespoon crème
   fraîche

ORANGE DRESSING
1 orange
2 teaspoons light soy
   sauce
1 tablespoon light olive oil

Scallops are one of nature's wonders: the sweet soft meat with a good caramelized outside is unbeatable as perfect seafood. I have paired them here with a fennel purée, and the aniseed flavors are heightened by the star anise in the five-spice powder.

To make the fennel purée, put the fennel, butter and stock in a saucepan over high heat and bring to a boil. Reduce the heat to low and simmer until the fennel is softened, about 20 minutes. Drain the fennel, reserving 1 tablespoon of the stock, and tip into a food processor or blender. Blitz with the reserved stock to a fine purée. Season with salt and pepper, add the crème fraîche and blitz again briefly to combine. Set aside.

To make the dressing, using a sharp knife, peel the orange, removing all the skin and pith, then carefully cut into sections, working over a bowl so any juice is caught. Cut the sections into slightly smaller pieces, then mix with the soy sauce, oil and juice in the bowl until well combined. Set aside.

Sprinkle the Chinese five-spice powder onto a plate. Pat the scallops dry with paper towels, then press both sides of each scallop into the powder and season them with salt.

Heat a frying pan over high heat and add the oil. Keeping the heat high, add the scallops and fry until golden brown, about 2½ minutes per side.

Put the scallops on top of the fennel purée, then sprinkle with the cress and drizzle the dressing over. Serve immediately.

Crab, Ginger & Coconut Crêpes

PREPARATION TIME: 15 minutes, plus 30 minutes resting time | COOKING TIME: 35 minutes | SERVES: 4

1 teaspoon sesame oil
1-inch piece of fresh gingerroot, peeled and finely chopped
11 ounces cooked crabmeat, flaked (about 2½ cups)
1 teaspoon soy sauce

CREPE BATTER
heaped 1 cup rice flour
1 cup coconut milk
1 teaspoon ground turmeric
1 tablespoon snipped chives, plus extra for sprinkling
a pinch of kosher salt
peanut oil, for frying

TO SERVE
2 tablespoons oyster sauce

When I make these, I am trying to recreate a dish I had in Malaysia. I love the coconut and turmeric-flavored batter and savory filling. You can use strips of pork instead of crab, and I sometimes add fresh herbs, shrimp and peanuts.

To make the crêpe batter, whisk together the rice flour, coconut milk, turmeric, chives and salt in a bowl with ½ cup water until thoroughly combined. Cover with plastic wrap and refrigerate for 30 minutes.

Preheat the oven to 275°F. To make the crêpes, heat an 8-inch frying pan over medium-high heat. Add 1–2 teaspoons peanut oil and, when it is hot, pour in one-quarter of the crêpe batter. Tilt the pan to spread the batter into a thin, lacy layer, then cook until the crêpe is set and the edges are starting to turn golden, about 5 minutes. Flip the crêpe over and cook until golden, 2–3 minutes longer. Turn the crêpe out onto a heatproof serving plate and keep warm in the oven while you cook the remaining three crêpes, adding more oil to the pan as required. Keep the crêpes warm.

Heat the sesame oil in a frying pan over medium heat. Add the ginger and cook, stirring often, for 2 minutes. Add the crabmeat and soy sauce and stir-fry until heated through. Remove from the heat.

Divide the crab mixture among the crêpes and roll them up. Serve immediately, with oyster sauce drizzled over and sprinkled with chives.

"I love the coconut- and turmeric-flavored batter and the flavorsome filling in these pancakes."

Tomato & Geranium Gelatins with Crab & Micro Basil

PREPARATION TIME: 20 minutes, plus overnight draining time and 4 hours setting time | COOKING TIME: 2 minutes | SERVES: 4

4½ pounds ripe tomatoes
1 small handful of basil
7 tablespoons white balsamic vinegar
7 tablespoons spring water
2 teaspoons sugar
1 teaspoon kosher salt
3 geranium leaves
8 gelatin sheets
11 ounces cooked crabmeat, flaked (about 2½ cups)
olive oil, for dressing
8 yellow cherry tomatoes, halved
8 red cherry tomatoes, halved

TO SERVE
1 small handful of micro purple basil

Although this may seem like a strange combination, tomatoes and geranium contain a similar chemical compound and so they really bring out the best in each other. This is a delicate gelatin made from the essence of tomato, then topped with a little crab. Perfect for a light summer dish.

Put the tomatoes, basil, white balsamic vinegar, spring water, sugar, salt and geranium leaves in a blender or food processor and blitz until finely chopped. Line a colander with a dampened piece of cheesecloth, then rest the colander over a large bowl so that it hangs with plenty of space in the bowl below it. Pour the tomato mix into the colander, cover with plastic wrap and let drain in the refrigerator overnight.

The next day, gently squeeze out the remaining juice from the tomato mix. Don't over-squeeze—you don't want any of the pulp, which would make the liquid cloudy. You need about 3 cups liquid. If there is less than this, don't dilute it by adding water. Instead, change the ingredient measurements to 2 cups liquid and 5 gelatin leaves.

Heat 1 cup of the tomato liquid in a saucepan until just boiling, then remove from the heat. Meanwhile, soak the gelatin sheets in cold water until softened, about 5 minutes, then squeeze to remove any excess water and stir into the heated tomato liquid until completely melted. Pour the tomato mix into the remaining tomato liquid and stir well. Divide among four soup bowls and refrigerate for 3–4 hours to set.

When you are ready to eat, dress the crab with a little olive oil, then pile it on the gelatins. Add the tomatoes and sprinkle with the micro basil before serving.

Lobster Rolls with Pea Shoots

PREPARATION TIME: 40 minutes, plus 1 hour freezing time and making the rolls and mayonnaise | COOKING TIME: 6 minutes | SERVES: 4

2 live lobsters, about
  1 pound 2 ounces each,
  or 1 pound 5 ounces
  cooked lobster meat
4 hotdog buns, made with
  the dough for Deluxe
  Burger Buns (see
  page 201)
Mayonnaise (see
  page 199)
kosher salt and freshly
  ground black pepper

These decadent rolls are perfect with a crisp white wine. You could fill them with shrimp too, which is just as good but far cheaper. If you don't want to make the rolls from my buttery sweet dough, you can use purchased brioche rolls, split and toasted.

If using live lobsters, put them in the freezer up to 1 hour before cooking. Bring a large pot of water to a boil, then add the lobsters and cook until the shells turn red. The cooking time will depend upon the size of the lobsters—the general rule is 10 minutes per pound. So, if you decide to use one larger lobster, calculate the cooking time accordingly. Remove the lobsters from the water and put on a tray to cool.

To remove the meat from the lobsters, take a large knife and insert the tip between the eyes of one of the lobsters, then draw the knife along the middle to cut it in half. Remove the tail meat and any extra little bits in the body. Pull off the claw and legs, crack them with a meat mallet or a large knife and remove the meat. Repeat this process with the second lobster.

Chop all the lobster meat into small pieces and put it in a bowl. Season with salt and pepper and add mayonnaise to taste. (If you want to make the mixture in advance, cover with plastic wrap and refrigerate.)

Split each bun lengthwise, keeping a "hinge" at one side. Spoon the lobster mixture into the buns, then serve.

Halloumi, Quinoa, Pomegranate & Mint Salad

PREPARATION TIME: 10 minutes, plus making the sauce | COOKING TIME: 30 minutes | SERVES: 4

heaped 1 cup quinoa
4 scallions, finely sliced
7 ounces pink radishes, finely sliced (about 1¾ cups)
1 large handful of mint leaves, roughly chopped
¼ cup chopped pistachios
⅓ cup pomegranate seeds
11 ounces halloumi cheese

DRESSING
juice of 1 lemon
3½ tablespoons olive oil
2 tablespoons pomegranate molasses

TO SERVE
Yogurt Sauce (see page 199) (optional)

I love the Middle-Eastern flavors of pomegranate, pistachios and mint, combined here with halloumi cheese. I have added quinoa, rather than the traditional bulgur wheat or couscous, to make it a more protein-based dish. The result is a jewel-like salad.

Put the quinoa into a saucepan and cook according to the package directions. (It is cooked just like rice, with the lid on and until the water is absorbed, and should take about 20 minutes.) Let cool.

Meanwhile, to make the dressing, whisk together all the ingredients until thoroughly combined. Set aside.

Tip the quinoa into a large mixing bowl. Add the scallions and radishes and mix to combine, then add the mint, pistachios, pomegranate seeds and dressing and toss well. (The salad can be made a few hours in advance, if more convenient; this will let the flavors develop.)

When you are ready to eat, heat a ridged grill pan over medium-high heat. Cut the halloumi into ½-inch-thick slices and pan-grill until soft and well marked with charred lines, about 3 minutes per side.

Pile the quinoa salad on individual plates and set the halloumi on top. Serve with Yogurt Sauce on the side, if desired.

Superfood Salad with Avocado & Lemon Dressings

PREPARATION TIME: 15 minutes | COOKING TIME: 5 minutes | SERVES: 4

7 ounces asparagus,
   trimmed
4 ounces mixed micro
   lettuce leaves
2 bulbs of fennel, very
   finely sliced
2 carrots, peeled
   and grated
6 ounces cooked beets,
   peeled and diced
   (about 1 cup)
Cooked Turkey (see page
   205) (optional)
the seeds tapped out
   of ½ pomegranate
¼ cup chopped
   macadamia nuts

AVOCADO DRESSING
2 ripe avocados
½ garlic clove, finely
   chopped
1 teaspoon olive oil
1 tablespoon plain yogurt
juice of 1 lemon
kosher salt and freshly
   ground black pepper

LEMON DRESSING
juice of 2 lemons
5 tablespoons olive oil

Liver-boosting beets, cleansing asparagus and iron-rich micro leaves, plus a dressing with the good fats of avocado and good bacteria of yogurt and olive oil, all topped off with crunchy macadamia nuts—what could be healthier?

Bring a pan of water to a boil and cook the asparagus until just tender, 4–6 minutes. Drain and refresh under cold water to stop the cooking process.

Meanwhile, make the avocado dressing by putting all the ingredients in a blender or food processor with 5 teaspoons water and blitzing until smooth. Season with salt and pepper. Also make the lemon dressing by whisking together the lemon juice and olive oil in a small bowl.

To assemble the salad you will need a large platter. Spread the micro lettuce leaves over the platter, then layer up the fennel, carrots, beets and asparagus, finishing with the turkey on top, if using. Pour the avocado dressing over the salad and sprinkle the pomegranate seeds and macadamia nuts over. Serve with the lemon dressing on the side.

Cauliflower & Onion Pakoras
with Mango & Fenugreek Salsa

PREPARATION TIME: 25 minutes, plus 15 minutes resting time | COOKING TIME: 30 minutes | SERVES: 4

11 ounces cauliflower
   florets (about 3 cups)
1¼ cups vegetable oil
2 red onions, sliced into
   thick rings

MANGO & FENUGREEK
SALSA
2 mangoes
1 shallot, finely diced
1 hot red chili, seeded and
   finely diced
½ teaspoon fenugreek
   seeds
3 tablespoons white wine
   vinegar
2 tablespoons packed
   brown sugar
1 teaspoon chopped
   cilantro leaves

BATTER
2 cups chickpea flour
1 teaspoon cumin seeds
½ teaspoon ground
   turmeric
½ teaspoon garam
   masala
juice of 1 lemon
kosher salt and freshly
   ground black pepper

These onion rings and cauliflower florets, coated in a spicy crisp chickpea-flour batter, are irresistible. The salsa is a modern touch that adds freshness to the dish.

To make the salsa, slice each mango down either side of the pit, using a sharp knife. On the inside of each slice, cut the flesh into squares, cutting down to the peel but not piercing it, and scoop out with a spoon. Peel the remaining parts of the mango and slice the flesh from the pit. Put the mango in a saucepan over medium-high heat with all the other salsa ingredients, except the cilantro, and bring to a boil. Reduce the heat to low and simmer until soft and fragrant, about 20 minutes. Let cool, then stir in the cilantro.

Meanwhile, to make the batter, mix the chickpea flour, spices and lemon juice together in a bowl until well combined, then add 1¼ cups water and beat until the batter is smooth and thick. Season with salt and pepper. Cover with plastic wrap and refrigerate for 15 minutes.

While the batter is resting, bring a large saucepan of water to a boil and blanch the cauliflower for 3 minutes. Drain in a colander and refresh under cold water. Let drain completely.

Heat the oil in a large, heavy-based saucepan over medium heat until hot. Take care not to overheat the oil—it will be hot enough when an onion ring dropped into the oil sizzles immediately.

Quickly dip half the blanched cauliflower and onion rings in the batter, a piece at a time, and slide into the oil. Deep-fry until golden and crisp, just a few minutes, then scoop out of the oil using a slotted spoon and drain on paper towels. Keep hot. Repeat with the remaining vegetables. (It is important not to cook too many pieces at the same time, because the oil temperature will drop.) Serve the pakoras hot with the salsa on the side.

Zucchini, Mozzarella & Basil Bruschetta

PREPARATION TIME: 10 minutes | COOKING TIME: 10 minutes | SERVES: 4

4 zucchini
1 tablespoon olive oil, plus extra for drizzling
½ teaspoon dried chili flakes
1 teaspoon grated lemon zest
4 slices of sourdough bread
1 large garlic clove, halved
2 balls of buffalo mozzarella cheese
1 small handful of basil leaves
kosher salt and freshly ground black pepper

Sometimes simple is good, but you need to use the best mozzarella and the freshest zucchini you can find for the topping, and good-quality bread finished off with the richest olive oil for the base. I love these as a light lunch or as pre-dinner nibbles with drinks.

Slice the zucchini lengthwise into thin ribbons using a swivel-bladed vegetable peeler. Heat the oil in a large frying pan over medium heat. Add the zucchini and chili flakes, and season with salt and pepper. Fry, stirring occasionally, until softened, about 10 minutes. Stir in the lemon zest and remove from the heat.

Meanwhile, heat the broiler and toast the sourdough slices (or toast them in a toaster). Rub the cut side of the garlic over one side of each slice.

Pile the zucchini ribbons on top of the sourdough slices. Tear up the mozzarella and put it on the zucchini. Sprinkle with the basil leaves and drizzle a little oil over. Serve immediately.

Roasted Portobello Mushroom & Garlic Cream Cheese Focaccias

PREPARATION TIME: 10 minutes | COOKING TIME: 25 minutes | SERVES: 4

4 tomatoes
4 portobello mushrooms, trimmed and peeled
4 garlic cloves, peeled
1 thyme sprig, leaves picked, plus extra thyme leaves for sprinkling
1 tablespoon olive oil
4 (4-inch) squares of focaccia
6 ounces garlic- and herb-flavored cream cheese (about 2/3 cup)
kosher salt and freshly ground black pepper

Vegetarians rejoice! Here, the heat of juicy, meaty mushrooms melts garlicky cream cheese, which is perfectly balanced by the sweetness of roasted tomatoes.

Preheat the oven to 400°F. Slice off the top and bottom from each tomato, then cut the tomatoes across into thick slices. Lay the mushrooms, gill side up, in a baking pan. Season with salt and pepper, then top each mushroom with a few slices of tomato. Crush the garlic cloves with the flat of a large knife and put one clove on each mushroom. Sprinkle with the thyme, season again and drizzle the oil over.

Roast the mushrooms until juicy and cooked through, 15–20 minutes. Remove from the oven and keep warm. Turn on the broiler.

Slice the focaccia squares horizontally in half and toast the cut sides under the broiler. Spread the toasted sides with a thick layer of cream cheese. Set a roasted mushroom on each of the bottom halves, removing the garlic cloves, if desired. Sprinkle with thyme leaves, then put the focaccia top halves in place and serve.

Beet Mousse with Creamy Goat Cheese

PREPARATION TIME: 20 minutes, plus overnight chilling time | COOKING TIME: 30 minutes | SERVES: 4

1 red onion, roughly chopped
14 ounces raw beets, peeled and quartered
1 garlic clove, peeled
6 tablespoons olive oil
1 teaspoon sugar
4 gelatin sheets
1 cup hot vegetable stock
1 tablespoon lemon juice
2 extra-large egg whites
7 ounces soft, rindless goat cheese
¼ cup heavy cream
kosher salt and freshly ground black pepper

TO SERVE
2 handfuls of red beet sprouts
toast triangles

Beets are a wonderful vegetable: their color, texture and flavor are great and they're also a healthy vegetable with liver-cleansing properties. Here I have made a brightly colored and deeply flavored beet mousse, which is delicious spread on toast.

Preheat the oven to 400°F. Put the onion, beets and garlic in a baking pan, drizzle the oil over and season with the sugar, salt and pepper. Cover with foil and cook until tender, about 30 minutes.

Soak the gelatin sheets in cold water until softened, about 5 minutes. Squeeze to remove any excess water, then put into a bowl with the hot stock and stir until melted. Let cool. Put the roasted beets, onion and garlic and the lemon juice in a blender or food processor and pour in the stock. Blitz until very fine, then check the seasoning.

Beat the egg whites in a large, clean bowl until soft peaks form. Using a large metal spoon, fold the egg whites into the beet mixture. Spoon the mousse into serving dishes and refrigerate overnight to set.

Just before serving, mix the goat cheese with the cream and spoon on top of each beet mousse. Sprinkle the red beet sprouts over the top and serve toast triangles on the side.

Twice-Baked Cheese Soufflés with a Tomato & Micro Basil Salad

PREPARATION TIME: 25 minutes, plus 10 minutes infusing time and 10 minutes chilling time |
COOKING TIME: 35 minutes | SERVES: 4

1 cup milk
1 onion, finely chopped
10 tablespoons (1 stick +
  2 tablespoons) butter
1/3 cup all-purpose flour
2 cups grated aged
  Cheddar cheese
1 teaspoon English
  mustard
1 teaspoon wholegrain
  mustard
3 extra-large eggs,
  separated
2/3 cup heavy cream
1/2 cup finely grated
  Parmesan cheese
kosher salt and freshly
  ground black pepper

TOMATO & MICRO BASIL
SALAD
4 ounces cherry
  tomatoes, quartered
5 teaspoons white
  balsamic vinegar
a pinch of sugar
1 large handful of
  micro basil

Put the milk and onion in a saucepan over medium heat and slowly bring to a boil. Remove from the heat immediately and let infuse for 10 minutes. Meanwhile, melt 7 tablespoons of the butter and brush four 5-ounce ramekins with some of the butter in a thick layer. Refrigerate the ramekins to set the butter, then brush with another layer of butter. Repeat until all the melted butter is used.

Strain the milk into a pitcher. Melt the remaining butter in a nonstick saucepan, add the flour and cook, stirring with a wooden spoon, for 1 minute. Using a whisk, gradually mix in the milk, whisking until smooth. Add the Cheddar cheese and both mustards, then remove from the heat and whisk in the egg yolks, one at a time. Season with salt and pepper. Let cool.

Preheat the oven to 350°F. Beat the egg whites in a large, clean bowl until stiff peaks form. Tip the egg whites onto the cooled cheese mixture and very gently fold through with a large metal spoon. Stir the mixture as little as possible to retain the maximum air.

Divide the soufflé mixture among the prepared ramekins and set them in a roasting pan. Pour boiling water into the pan to come two-thirds of the way up the sides of the ramekins. Bake the soufflés until risen and golden brown, about 15 minutes. Remove the pan from the oven and the ramekins from the water bath and let them cool completely—the soufflés will collapse. (Note: You can prepare the recipe to this stage a few hours in advance.)

Increase the oven temperature to 400°F. Unmold the soufflés into four small oven-to-table dishes. Pour the cream over the top of the soufflés and sprinkle with the Parmesan. Bake until golden and crisp, about 15 minutes.

Meanwhile, make the salad by tossing together all the ingredients in a bowl until well combined. Serve the soufflés immediately, with the salad.

"These are fail-safe soufflés that anyone can make!"

Main Meals

Chicken & Lemongrass Skewers with Carrot & Cucumber Salad

PREPARATION TIME: 25 minutes, plus 15 minutes marinating time | COOKING TIME: 10 minutes | SERVES: 4

4 boneless, skinless chicken breast halves, cut into bite-size pieces
1 teaspoon ground turmeric
2 teaspoons sugar
1 teaspoon soy sauce
1 hot red chili, seeded and finely chopped
1 small handful of micro cilantro
1 teaspoon Thai red curry paste
8 lemongrass stalks, outer leaves removed and ends cut off
oil, for greasing
kosher salt and freshly ground black pepper

CARROT & CUCUMBER SALAD
2 carrots, peeled and cut into very thin slices
½ hothouse cucumber or 2 Lebanese cucumbers, cut into very thin slices
2 scallions, cut into fine 2-inch-long strips
1 hot red chili, seeded and finely diced
1 small handful of micro cilantro
juice of 1 lime

TO SERVE
steamed basmati rice

Southeast Asian cuisine is a balance of three factors—sweet, sour and hot—so the first rule is to master that. Then when you get used to the basic ingredients (chili, fish sauce, lime, cilantro, ginger, garlic, lemongrass and kaffir limes), you can experiment and make some amazingly aromatic dishes.

Put the chicken, turmeric, sugar, soy sauce, chili, cilantro and curry paste in a blender or food processor, season generously with salt and pepper and blitz to a smooth paste. Divide the paste into eight portions and shape each one around a lemongrass stalk, covering two-thirds of it and leaving a gap at one end as a handle. Cover with plastic wrap and set aside.

To make the salad, toss together all the ingredients in a bowl until thoroughly combined. Season with salt and pepper. Cover with plastic wrap and refrigerate for about 15 minutes to let the flavors develop.

When you are ready to eat, heat the broiler. Lay the chicken skewers on a lightly greased broiler pan and broil, 4–5 inches from the heat, until cooked through and golden, about 5 minutes per side. Serve the skewers immediately, with the salad and rice.

Chicken Breast with Hazelnut & Jerusalem Artichoke Couscous

PREPARATION TIME: 20 minutes | **COOKING TIME:** 20 minutes | **SERVES:** 4

7 ounces Jerusalem artichokes, peeled and cut into small pieces (about 1½ cups)
2 tablespoons olive oil
4 boneless chicken breast halves
¾ cup couscous
1¼ cups chicken stock
4 tablespoons butter
1 red onion, finely chopped
1 teaspoon finely chopped chives, plus extra for garnish
2 heaped tablespoons chopped flat-leaf parsley
scant ½ cup roughly chopped hazelnuts

DRESSING
5 tablespoons olive oil
5 teaspoons hazelnut oil
2 tablespoons cider vinegar
a pinch of sugar
kosher salt and freshly ground black pepper

Couscous is really easy to prepare and is also a great vessel for different flavors. While often paired with Middle-Eastern or North-African flavors, here it has an earthy nutty freshness to it, rounded off with a hazelnut-oil dressing.

Preheat the oven to 400°F. Put the Jerusalem artichokes in a baking dish, drizzle the oil over and season with salt and pepper. Roast until cooked and lightly browned, about 20 minutes.

Meanwhile, heat a frying pan over medium-high heat. Season the chicken breasts on both sides with salt and pepper, then put the breasts, skin-side down, in the pan. Cook until golden all over, about 7 minutes. Transfer to a baking pan, skin-side up, and put into the oven with the artichokes. Roast until cooked through, about 10 minutes. To test if they are done, insert the tip of a sharp knife into the thickest part of a breast—the juices should run clear.

While the artichokes and chicken are roasting, put the couscous in a large bowl. Bring the stock to a boil, then pour it over the couscous and fork through. Cover with plastic wrap and let steam until the stock has been absorbed, about 5 minutes. Fork the couscous again.

Remove the chicken and artichokes from the oven. Set the chicken to one side. Add the butter, onion, chives, parsley, hazelnuts and roasted artichokes to the couscous and toss well.

In a small bowl, whisk together all the dressing ingredients until thoroughly combined. Pour half the dressing into the couscous and mix well. Season the couscous with salt and pepper.

Slice each of the chicken breasts against the grain on the diagonal and arrange on top of the couscous. Pour the remaining dressing over and serve sprinkled with chives.

Saffron-Poached Chicken with Parsley & Tarragon Gremolata

PREPARATION TIME: 25 minutes | COOKING TIME: 40 minutes | SERVES: 4

2½ cups chicken stock

⅔ cup white wine

a large pinch of saffron threads

4 boneless, skinless chicken breast halves

8 baby carrots, trimmed

4 bulbs of baby fennel, trimmed and cut in half

4 scallions, trimmed

2 zucchini, cut into ¼-inch-thick batons

kosher salt and freshly ground black pepper

TARRAGON GREMOLATA

scant ⅓ cup finely chopped flat-leaf parsley

1 teaspoon grated orange zest

1 teaspoon grated lemon zest

1 small handful of tarragon

1 garlic clove, finely chopped

3½ tablespoons olive oil

TO SERVE

boiled new potatoes

Saffron adds such a wonderful perfume and color to dishes. Here I have gently poached some chicken and vegetables in a saffron-infused stock, then added extra layers of flavors with the Italian classic gremolata, adding orange zest for extra aroma.

Pour the stock and wine into a saucepan and bring to a boil. Add the saffron threads, then reduce the heat to low and simmer for 5 minutes.

Meanwhile, to make the gremolata, put all the ingredients in a bowl and mix to combine. Season with salt and pepper and set aside.

Season the chicken with salt and pepper. Bring the stock back to a boil, then put the chicken in the stock, reduce the heat to low again and simmer until cooked through, about 10 minutes. Remove the chicken from the stock, cover with foil and let rest in a warm place.

Meanwhile, put the carrots, fennel, scallions and zucchini in the stock and cook for 5 minutes. Use a slotted spoon to remove the vegetables from the stock and keep warm. Increase the heat and simmer the stock until it is reduced by half, 15–20 minutes.

Cut each of the chicken breasts into slices against the grain on the diagonal. Divide the vegetables among individual deep plates and put the chicken slices on top. Spoon a little stock over and add spoonfuls of gremolata. Serve immediately with boiled new potatoes, if desired.

Chicken Breast Stuffed with Ricotta & Watercress

PREPARATION TIME: 10 minutes | COOKING TIME: 35 minutes | SERVES: 4

8 ounces ricotta cheese
   (1 cup)
a large pinch of freshly
   grated nutmeg
1 cup watercress
14 ounces small boiling
   potatoes
6 ounces cherry tomatoes
   (about 1 cup)
2 red onions, quartered
2 garlic cloves, peeled
1 tablespoon olive oil
4 boneless, skinless
   chicken breast halves
kosher salt and freshly
   ground pepper

TO SERVE
arugula
crusty bread

This is a really easy one-pan wonder of a dish. You can use all sorts of cheese to stuff the chicken: feta works well, as does garlicky goat cheese. It's a rustic and colorful dish.

Preheat the oven to 400°F. Mix together the ricotta and nutmeg in a bowl and season with salt and pepper. Set a saucepan over medium-low heat and wilt the watercress with a splash of water, then drain off any liquid and mix the watercress into the ricotta.

Put the potatoes, tomatoes, onions and garlic in a baking dish. Drizzle the oil over and season with salt and pepper.

Lay the chicken breasts on a cutting board. Cut each one open horizontally along the middle, keeping them "hinged" along one edge. Open out each breast to make a butterfly shape. Divide the ricotta mixture among the breasts, spreading it across both halves of each. Roll up, securing the stuffed breasts closed with one or two wooden toothpicks.

Set the chicken on top of the vegetables in the baking dish. Bake until the chicken is cooked through, about 30 minutes. To test if the chicken is done, insert the tip of a knife into the thickest part of one of the breasts—the juices should run clear.

Slice each stuffed breast thickly on the diagonal and place on a plate with the vegetables. Serve with arugula and crusty bread.

Roast Chicken with Salsa Verde

PREPARATION TIME: 20 minutes, plus 20 minutes resting time | COOKING TIME: 1 hour 35 minutes | SERVES: 4

1 roaster chicken, about
  3 pounds 5 ounces
1 lemon, halved
1 onion, peeled
olive oil, for drizzling
4 garlic cloves, peeled
1 butternut squash, about
  1 pound 2 ounces,
  halved, seeded, peeled
  and cut into wedges
a pinch of dried chili
  flakes
9 ounces broccoli, or more
  if desired
kosher salt and freshly
  ground black pepper

SALSA VERDE
2 canned anchovy fillets
  in oil, drained
1 garlic clove, peeled
grated zest and juice
  of 1 lemon
1 tablespoon baby capers,
  drained
1 large handful of mixed
  herbs, such as tarragon,
  parsley and mint,
  roughly chopped
scant ½ cup olive oil

Roast chicken is always an easy family dish, but sometimes I crave a variation. Here I have roasted it with butternut squash, served it with some green veggies and made a super-charged salsa verde dressing to accompany it.

Preheat the oven to 475°F. Rinse the chicken inside and out under cold water and pat dry with paper towels. Season the chicken with salt and pepper, then stuff the cavity with the lemon halves and onion. Put the chicken in a roasting pan, drizzle a little oil over and put into the oven. After 15 minutes, turn the temperature down to 375°F and continue roasting the chicken until cooked through, about 1¼ hours. To test if the chicken is done, insert the tip of a knife into the thickest part of the breast meat near the leg—the juices should run clear. An instant-read thermometer should register 180°F.

About 30 minutes before the chicken has finished roasting, crush the garlic cloves with the flat side of a knife and put them around the chicken along with the butternut squash. Drizzle a little oil over the squash, sprinkle with the chili flakes and season with salt and pepper.

Meanwhile, make the salsa verde: Using a mortar and pestle or mini blender, crush the anchovies and garlic together. Tip into a bowl and add the lemon zest and juice, baby capers, herbs and oil. Stir until well combined. Season with salt and pepper and set aside.

When the chicken is done, remove from the oven, cover with foil and let rest for 20 minutes. Shortly before it is time to eat, cook the broccoli in salted boiling water until al dente. Carve the chicken and serve with the broccoli and butternut squash, with the salsa verde drizzled over the top.

Chicken & Tamarind Stir-Fry with Mustard-Seed Rice

PREPARATION TIME: 15 minutes | COOKING TIME: 40 minutes | SERVES: 4

1 tablespoon vegetable oil
4 boneless, skinless chicken breast halves, cut into bite-size pieces
6 ounces sugar snap peas
1 red bell pepper, seeded and diced
4 scallions, trimmed and cut into 1-inch-long pieces
2 garlic cloves, thinly sliced
1 small handful of purple basil leaves, roughly chopped
kosher salt and freshly ground black pepper

MUSTARD-SEED RICE
1 teaspoon vegetable oil
1 shallot, chopped
1½ cups basmati rice
2 teaspoons yellow mustard seeds
½ teaspoon ground turmeric

TAMARIND SAUCE
1 teaspoon tamarind syrup, or 2 teaspoons tamarind paste soaked in 2 tablespoons water, then strained
½ teaspoon each hot chili powder and cracked black pepper
1 tablespoon soy sauce
1 teaspoon fish sauce
1 teaspoon sugar

Stir-fries are great quick supper dishes. You can throw in all sorts of vegetables and season to your own taste. I have used tamarind here for a touch of sourness, which you can buy in syrup or paste form in Asian markets and many supermarkets.

To make the mustard-seed rice, heat the oil in a frying pan over medium-low heat, add the shallot and fry gently until softened and translucent, about 5 minutes. Add the rice and mustard seeds, then pour in 2½ cups water. Add the turmeric, season with salt and pepper and stir to combine. Increase the heat to high and bring to a boil, then reduce the heat to low, cover and simmer until the water has been absorbed and the rice is cooked through, about 20 minutes. Set aside, covered, while cooking the stir-fry.

Meanwhile, to make the tamarind sauce, mix together all the ingredients in a small bowl until well combined.

Heat the oil in a wok or frying pan over high heat. When the wok is very hot, add the chicken, season with salt and pepper and stir-fry for 5 minutes. Add the sugar snap peas, red pepper and scallions and cook for another 5 minutes, then add the garlic and cook for 3 minutes longer. Stir in the prepared tamarind sauce and the purple basil. When heated through, serve immediately with the Mustard-Seed Rice.

Pan-Roasted Duck with Figs, Red Chard & Peppercorn Sauce

PREPARATION TIME: 15 minutes, plus 10 minutes resting time and making the mash (optional |
COOKING TIME: 40 minutes | SERVES: 4

4 duck breasts
4 figs, quartered
2 teaspoons brown sugar
1 teaspoon pink
    peppercorns
scant ½ cup Madeira
2 tablespoons butter
4 ounces red chard,
    stalks and leaves
    separated and chopped
kosher salt and freshly
    ground black pepper

TO SERVE
Celery-Root Mash (see
    page 205) (optional)

Duck is an excellent meat. It has had a bad press for being too fatty, but when cooked like this—slowly, skin side down—it is beautiful. The figs are oozing with fragrant sweetness and the pink peppercorns (which are actually berries) add a delicate spiciness.

Preheat the oven to 350°F. Finely score the skin on the duck breasts with the tip of a sharp knife and season generously with salt and pepper. Heat an ovenproof frying pan over low heat, then lay the duck breasts, skin-side down, in the pan. Slowly cook the duck for 10–15 minutes, draining off the fat as it accumulates, until the skin starts to turn crisp. Turn up the heat and cook until the skin is browned and crisp all over, then flip the breasts over and cook for 2 minutes longer. Transfer to the oven to roast until the breasts are firm to the touch but still quite pink inside, about 5 minutes. Remove from the oven, cover with foil and let rest for 10 minutes.

Meanwhile, drain any remaining fat from the pan, leaving behind the sediment. Set the pan over medium heat, add the figs and brown sugar, and cook until caramelized, 3–4 minutes. Add the peppercorns and cook for 1 more minute, then add the Madeira and simmer until the sauce is reduced and thickened, about 5 minutes longer.

Melt the butter in a separate pan, add the chard stalks and cook for 3–4 minutes, then add the leaves and cook until wilted and tender, 1–2 minutes.

Slice the duck against the grain on the diagonal and serve with the chard and caramelized figs. Drizzle the peppercorn sauce over and serve Celery-Root Mash on the side, if desired.

Miso-Glazed Pork Belly with Stir-Fried Bok Choy

PREPARATION TIME: 25 minutes, plus overnight salting time | COOKING TIME: 2½ hours | SERVES: 4

scant 1 cup coarse sea salt
¾ cup sugar
1 piece of skin-on pork
  belly, about 3 pounds
  5 ounces
MISO GLAZE
scant ½ cup mirin
¼ cup sugar
2 tablespoons miso paste

BOK CHOY
1 teaspoon toasted
  sesame oil
4 large heads of bok
  choy, quartered, or
  8 small heads of bok
  choy, halved
1 hot red chili, minced
1 tablespoon soy sauce

TO SERVE
steamed rice

Pork belly is a fantastic cut: it's cheap and has great flavor. It works really well with Asian ingredients and here I have cooked it with a miso glaze. The sweetness and saltiness really work well together. The rice and bok choy keep the rest of the flavors balanced.

Stir the salt and sugar in a large measure with 2 cups warm water until dissolved. Put the pork belly in a deep bowl or baking dish and pour the salty mixture over. Cover with plastic wrap and refrigerate overnight.

Preheat the oven to 350°F. Drain the pork belly and set it on a rack in a roasting pan. Pour enough boiling water into the pan to come 1 inch up the sides. Cover the pan with foil and roast the pork until it is very tender, about 2 hours.

To make the miso glaze, put the mirin and sugar in a saucepan over medium heat and bring to a boil. Stir in the miso paste, then remove the pan from the heat and continue stirring until smooth. Set aside.

Remove the pork from the oven and increase the temperature to 400°F. Brush the miso glaze over the pork until well coated, then return to the oven and roast, uncovered, until the glaze is glistening and sticky, about 30 minutes.

Meanwhile, for the bok choy, heat the sesame oil in a large frying pan, add the bok choy and stir-fry until starting to wilt, about 5 minutes. Add the chili and soy sauce and continue cooking for a few more minutes.

Remove the pork belly from the oven, slice it against the grain and place on plates with the bok choy. Serve with rice.

"I love the wintery flavors of chestnut and quince with a touch of cinnamon: comfort food at its best."

Pork, Quince & Chestnut Casserole with Watercress Mash

PREPARATION TIME: 20 minutes | COOKING TIME: 1½ hours | SERVES: 4

2 tablespoons olive oil
1 piece of boneless
  fresh pork leg, about
  1 pound 10 ounces, cut
  into bite-size cubes
scant ½ cup white wine
2 onions, cut into wedges
2 quinces, peeled and
  sliced
9 ounces canned or
  vacuum-packed
  chestnuts
1 cinnamon stick
2 cups vegetable stock
1 sage sprig, leaves
  picked, plus extra
  for garnish

WATERCRESS MASH
1 pound 5 ounces
  potatoes, peeled and
  cut into chunks
1 tablespoon olive oil
6 ounces watercress,
  roughly chopped
  (about 1½ cups)
kosher salt and freshly
  ground black pepper

Although we often think of Greek food as being very summery, with lots of salads and fish, in the winter it comes into its own in a different way. This casserole was inspired by winters in Greece, sitting by the log fire looking at views of the snow on the mountains.

Heat 1 tablespoon of the oil in a large frying pan over high heat. Add the pork, in batches, season with salt and pepper and sear until well browned all over. You want a good color, as it adds flavor later. It will take 15–20 minutes to sear all the pork. After the last batch is done and removed from the pan, pour in the wine to deglaze the pan, swishing the wine around and scraping the bits of pork off the bottom for about 4 minutes. Set the pan aside.

In a heavy pot or casserole, heat the remaining oil over medium heat. Add the onions and quinces and cook, stirring occasionally, for 5 minutes, then add the chestnuts, cinnamon stick, pork and deglazed juices from the frying pan. Add the stock and sage leaves and bring to a boil. Reduce the heat to low and simmer until the pork is tender, about 1 hour. Season with salt and pepper.

About 30 minutes before the pork is done, put the potatoes in a large saucepan, cover with water and bring to a boil. Turn the heat down to low, cover and simmer until tender, about 20 minutes. Drain the potatoes in a colander and let steam-dry for a few minutes, then return to the pan. Add the oil and watercress to the pan and mash with the potato. Season with salt and pepper. Serve the pork casserole sprinkled with sage leaves, with the watercress mash on the side.

Smoked Tea- & Star-Anise-Braised Pork Ribs with Pickled Cucumber

PREPARATION TIME: 15 minutes, plus 10 minutes pickling time | COOKING TIME: 2 hours | SERVES: 4

2 quarts vegetable stock
2-inch piece of fresh gingerroot, peeled and sliced
2 tablespoons Russian caravan or lapsang souchong tea leaves
3 star anise
2¼ pounds pork ribs, cut into individual ribs

PICKLED CUCUMBER
scant ⅓ cup white wine vinegar
2 teaspoons sugar
1 teaspoon kosher salt
1 hothouse cucumber, seeded and thinly sliced crosswise

GLAZE
1 teaspoon Chinese five-spice powder
1 tablespoon brown sugar
2 tablespoons soy sauce
2 tablespoons honey
1 teaspoon toasted sesame oil

TO SERVE
boiled rice (optional)

Cooking with tea is really interesting. Here, the tea leaves in the stock give the ribs a smoky, earthy depth. The pickled cucumber is brilliant and goes with many dishes, including Miso-Glazed Pork Belly (see page 92).

Pour the stock into a large saucepan and add the ginger, tea leaves and star anise. Bring to a boil, then reduce the heat to low and simmer for 5 minutes. Add the pork ribs, cover and simmer until cooked through, about 1 hour.

To make the pickled cucumber, put the vinegar and sugar in a saucepan and bring to a boil. Reduce the heat to low and simmer, stirring, until the sugar has dissolved. Remove from the heat and let cool completely. Meanwhile, mix together the salt and cucumber in a bowl and leave for 10 minutes, then tip the cucumber into a colander. Rinse off the salt under cold water and drain well. Return the cucumber to the bowl. Pour the cooled vinegar mixture over and toss well. Set aside.

To make the glaze, put all the ingredients in a small saucepan over medium heat and bring to a boil. Reduce the heat to low and simmer for 5 minutes. Remove from the heat and set aside.

Preheat the oven to 400°F. When the ribs are done, remove them from the pan and drain in a colander. (You don't need the liquid for this recipe, but don't discard it, as it is a great stock for Asian soups.) Put the ribs in a shallow baking pan and brush generously with the glaze. Roast, occasionally brushing with extra glaze, until sticky and well cooked, about 45 minutes. Remove the ribs from the oven and serve with the pickled cucumber and boiled rice, if desired.

Pulled BBQ Pork with Red Cabbage Slaw

PREPARATION TIME: 25 minutes, plus 15 minutes resting time plus making the sauce and mayonnaise |
COOKING TIME: 3 hours | SERVES: 4

olive oil, for oiling and
    drizzling
2 teaspoons smoked
    paprika
½ teaspoon ground cumin
½ teaspoon ground
    coriander
1 teaspoon ground
    turmeric
1 teaspoon dried oregano
2 teaspoons garlic salt
1 teaspoon celery salt
1 pork shoulder roast,
    about 3 pounds 5 ounces
scant ½ cup BBQ Sauce
    (see page 198)
1 tablespoon maple syrup
14 ounces sweet potatoes,
    cut into wedges
kosher salt and freshly
    ground black pepper

RED CABBAGE SLAW
½ small head of red
    cabbage, cored and
    finely sliced
2 carrots, peeled and
    grated
2 red apples, peeled,
    cored and grated
2 tablespoons Mayonnaise
    (see page 199)
1 small red onion, finely
    chopped

TO SERVE
Deluxe Burger Buns (see
    page 201) (optional)

I have an almost obsessional craving for barbecue dishes, such as pulled pork, ribs and so on. This is my pulled pork recipe, which I have made a little fresher by serving it with a red cabbage and apple slaw. Sweet potato wedges also go well with it.

Preheat the oven to 320°F and oil a baking dish. Mix together all the spices with the oregano, garlic salt and celery salt in a small bowl. Rub this all over the pork roast. Put the pork in the oiled baking dish, cover with foil and set on the middle rack in the oven. Roast for 1 hour, undisturbed. Pour about ½ cup water into the dish, then cover again and roast for 1½ hours longer.

Meanwhile, make the slaw. Toss together all the ingredients in a large bowl and season with salt and pepper. Cover with plastic wrap and refrigerate.

After the pork has been in the oven for 2½ hours, whisk the bbq sauce and maple syrup together in a small bowl and brush over the pork. Return to the oven uncovered for a final 30 minutes of roasting. Meanwhile, spread the sweet potato wedges on a baking sheet, drizzle some oil over and season with salt and pepper. Put into the oven on the rack below the pork.

When the pork is done, remove from the oven, cover with foil and let rest for 15 minutes. Leave the sweet potato wedges in the oven until you are ready to serve.

Shred the pork meat into small pieces using two forks and pile up on a serving platter. Serve immediately with the red cabbage slaw and sweet potato wedges and with the burger buns, if you like.

Rack of Lamb with Macadamia & Basil Crust

PREPARATION TIME: 25 minutes | COOKING TIME: 25 minutes | SERVES: 4

3 tablespoons olive oil
2 lean racks of lamb,
   French trimmed
12 asparagus spears
5 ounces mizuna, broken
   into the natural leaves
5 teaspoons balsamic
   vinegar

MACADAMIA & BASIL
CRUST
$1^2/_3$ cups macadamia nuts
2 tablespoons chopped
   basil leaves
2 cups fresh bread
   crumbs
10 tablespoons (1 stick +
   2 tablespoons) butter,
   cubed
kosher salt and freshly
   ground black pepper

TO SERVE
crushed and buttered
   boiled small potatoes

Rack of lamb is a very impressive cut of meat to serve for a special dinner. I've kept the rest of the dish very light, with mizuna leaves mixed with lightly cooked asparagus. The lamb also goes well with little crushed potatoes tossed in butter.

Preheat the oven to 400°F. To make the macadamia and basil crust, put all the ingredients in a blender or food processor and blitz until coarse-fine. Season with salt and pepper, then briefly blitz again.

Heat 1 tablespoon of the oil in a heavy-based frying pan over medium-high heat. Add the lamb and cook, turning occasionally, until golden brown all over, about 8 minutes. (You aren't cooking the lamb through at this stage.)

Put the lamb racks, fat-side up, in a roasting pan. Spread the macadamia and basil crust over the fat, pressing it down firmly. Roast for 10 minutes—the meat should still be pink inside. Remove from the oven and let rest in a warm place.

Meanwhile, bring a wide pan of salted water to a boil. Drop in the asparagus and cook until al dente, about 5 minutes. Put the mizuna in a bowl and dress with the remaining 2 tablespoons of oil and the balsamic vinegar. Add the asparagus spears and toss together.

Cut each lamb rack between the bones into individual chops and serve with crushed boiled potatoes and the mizuna and asparagus salad.

Lamb Skewers with Lentil Salad

PREPARATION TIME: 35 minutes, plus 8 hours marinating time or overnight, 10 minutes infusing and making the sauce and flatbreads | COOKING TIME: 15 minutes | SERVES: 4

½ onion, grated
2 garlic cloves, crushed
grated zest and juice of
 ½ lemon
a pinch of saffron threads
14 ounces boneless leg of
 lamb, cut into chunks
5 teaspoons olive oil
kosher salt and freshly
 ground black pepper

SALAD
6 radishes, finely sliced
½ hothouse cucumber or
 2 Lebanese cucumbers,
 finely sliced
4 scallions, finely sliced
¾ cup drained canned
 lentils
1 handful of flat-leaf
 parsley leaves
1 handful of mint leaves
2 heads of baby romaine,
 separated into leaves
½ teaspoon sumac
juice of 1 lemon
5 teaspoons olive oil

TO SERVE
Yogurt Sauce
 (see page 199)
4 plain Flatbreads
 (see page 202)

This dish was inspired by my travels in the Middle East. The marinade harks back to Persian cooking methods and the salad has its roots in Lebanese cuisine. In fact, the salad is very similar to fattoush, with the inclusion of tart, citrus-flavored sumac.

Put the onion, garlic, lemon zest and juice, and saffron in a large bowl and mix together. Let infuse for 10 minutes, then add the lamb and oil, and season with salt and pepper. Toss until the lamb is well coated with the marinade. Cover with plastic wrap and let marinate in the refrigerator for 8 hours or overnight.

When you are ready to cook the lamb, soak eight wooden skewers in cold water. Mix all the salad ingredients in a large bowl and toss until the leaves are well coated with lemon juice and oil. Cover with plastic wrap and refrigerate while you cook the lamb.

Put a ridged grill pan over high heat. Thread the lamb cubes onto the soaked wooden skewers and season with salt and pepper. When the pan is very hot, add the lamb skewers and pan-grill on all sides until the meat is done to your taste: it will take 10–12 minutes in total for the lamb to be pink inside and golden brown on the outside. Serve the skewers with the salad, some flatbreads and yogurt sauce on the side.

Sour Cherry Meatballs with Buttery Tagliatelle

PREPARATION TIME: 20 minutes | COOKING TIME: 45 minutes | SERVES: 4

9 ounces ground veal
   (heaped 1 cup)
9 ounces ground lamb
   (heaped 1 cup)
²/₃ cup dried sour cherries
   or dried cranberries
heaped ¹/₃ cup pine nuts,
   toasted
1 teaspoon ground
   allspice
½ teaspoon ground
   cinnamon
½ cup fresh bread
   crumbs
1 egg, beaten
2 tablespoons olive oil
7 tablespoons butter
2 onions, roughly chopped
scant ½ cup white wine
1 tablespoon chopped
   flat-leaf parsley
9 ounces tagliatelle
kosher salt and freshly
   ground black pepper

These meatballs are a little different from the usual recipes. The pine nuts and sour cherries, with an added touch of spice, give them an exotic taste, and the buttery noodles soak up the flavors.

Put the veal, lamb, sour cherries, pine nuts, spices, bread crumbs and egg in a large bowl. Season generously with salt and pepper and mix together well. Shape the mixture into 16 small balls.

Heat 1 tablespoon of the oil with 2 tablespoons of the butter in a large frying pan over medium heat. Add the onions and cook for 5 minutes, then reduce the heat to low and continue cooking until softened and caramelized, about 30 minutes longer.

About 10 minutes before the onions are done, heat the remaining oil with 1 tablespoon butter in another frying pan over medium-high heat. Add the meatballs and fry until browned all over and cooked through, about 10 minutes. Tip the meatballs in with the onions. Add the wine and cook for 10 minutes, then add the remaining butter and the parsley and stir through.

Meanwhile, set a large pot of water over high heat, add a large pinch of salt and bring to a rapid boil. Add the tagliatelle and cook according to the package directions, until al dente. Drain the tagliatelle in a colander, then add to the pan with the onions and meatballs. Season with salt and pepper, stir and serve.

"Meatballs have been done a million times, but these have another dimension of taste."

Pan-Grilled Rib Eye, Caramelized Shallots & Micro Watercress

PREPARATION TIME: 15 minutes | COOKING TIME: 30 minutes | SERVES: 4

1 teaspoon olive oil, plus extra for dressing
2 tablespoons butter
14 ounces shallots, ends trimmed
1 teaspoon sugar
3½ tablespoons balsamic vinegar
4 rib-eye steaks
7 ounces micro watercress
kosher salt and freshly ground black pepper

TO SERVE
shoestring fries or French fries (optional)

Classic flavor combos exist for a reason, and there is no doubt that the best way to serve a steak is with some caramelized onions and a peppery watercress salad. Get your grill pan as hot as possible and season the steak well.

Heat the oil and butter in a frying pan over low heat. Add the shallots, cover and cook very gently until golden brown, softened and caramelized, about 20 minutes. Stir in the sugar and balsamic vinegar and continue cooking, uncovered, until the liquid is reduced and sticky, about 10 minutes longer.

While the shallots are cooking, heat a ridged grill pan over high heat and season the steaks generously with salt and pepper. When the pan is hot, pan-grill the steaks to the desired degree of doneness, or about 4 minutes per side for medium-rare. Meanwhile, put the micro watercress in a bowl and dress with a splash of oil.

Serve the steaks with the caramelized shallots spooned on top and the dressed micro watercress on the side, accompanied by fries, if desired.

My Ultimate Hamburgers

PREPARATION TIME: 40 minutes, plus making the buns, mayonnaise and chutney | COOKING TIME: 15 minutes | MAKES: 8

2 teaspoons olive oil, plus extra for frying the burgers if needed
1 large shallot, finely diced
14 ounces rib-eye steak or boneless beef chuck, cut into chunks
1 egg
1 teaspoon Worcestershire sauce
1 tablespoon ketchup
4 bacon slices
8 slices of Cheddar cheese
½ head of crisp lettuce, shredded
8 Deluxe Burger Buns (see page 201), split in half
Garlic Mayonnaise (see page 199)
4 large dill pickles, sliced
2 tomatoes, sliced
1 recipe quantity Quick Tomato Chutney (see page 200)
kosher salt and freshly ground black pepper

So, claiming that my burgers are the ULTIMATE, ever, is quite a serious statement, but I stand by it. Customize at will, making them your personal, ultimate burgers. You can flavor the mayonnaise with wholegrain mustard or even truffle oil, or add blue cheese, Gruyère or even fried onions to your burger. The options are endless, and the perfect burger is just waiting to be made...

Heat the oil in a small frying pan over medium heat, then add the shallot and cook until softened and translucent, about 5 minutes. Remove from the heat and let cool.

Put the beef in a food processor and blitz until ground. Add the cooked shallot, egg, Worcestershire sauce and ketchup and season generously with salt and pepper. Pulse to combine. Shape the mixture into eight small patties. Cover with plastic wrap and refrigerate.

Heat a frying pan over medium heat and fry the bacon until cooked and slightly crisp, about 5 minutes. Remove with tongs and drain on paper towels, then break each slice in half; set aside. Add a little oil to the bacon fat in the frying pan, if needed, then add the beef patties. Cook to the desired degree of doneness, or 4–5 minutes per side for juicy patties that are still pink inside. About 1–2 minutes before you think the patties will be done, put a slice of cheese on top of each one.

Mix the lettuce with some garlic mayonnaise in a bowl, adjusting the amount used to taste, and divide among the bun bases. Put slices of pickle on the lettuce, followed by tomato and bacon and then a burger. Spread a spoonful of chutney over the inside of the bun tops, then close the burgers and serve.

Marinated Hanger Steak with Sweet Potato Mash & Cilantro-Honey Dressing

PREPARATION TIME: 25 minutes, plus 1 hour marinating time | COOKING TIME: 20 minutes | SERVES: 4

2 tablespoons soy sauce
2 garlic cloves, finely
  chopped
1 tablespoon olive oil
scant ½ cup pineapple
  juice
2 hanger steaks, about
  1 pound 2 ounces each
1 pound 2 ounces sweet
  potatoes, peeled
  and cut into chunks

CILANTRO-HONEY
DRESSING
1 hot red chili, seeded and
  roughly chopped
1 small handful of cilantro
juice of 1 lemon
1 teaspoon honey
2 tablespoons olive oil
kosher salt and freshly
  ground black pepper

Hanger steak is a great cut that is full of flavor when served rare, so adjust the cooking time suggested according to the thickness of your steaks. Here I have paired it with sweet potatoes and a light dressing similar to South America's chimichurri sauce.

Mix the soy sauce, garlic, oil and pineapple juice in a measure until well combined. Lay the hanger steaks in a flat dish and pour the soy mixture over. Roll the steaks in the marinade until well coated, then cover with plastic wrap and let marinate in the refrigerator for 1 hour.

Put the sweet potatoes in a saucepan, cover with lightly salted water and bring to a boil. Reduce the heat to low, cover and simmer until cooked through, about 20 minutes. Drain well, then mash with a little salt and pepper. Keep hot.

While the sweet potatoes are cooking, heat a ridged grill pan over medium-high heat. Remove the steaks from the marinade, pat dry with paper towels and season generously with salt and pepper. Put the steaks in the hot pan and pan-grill, turning often, until well browned on both sides but still quite pink in the middle, 8–10 minutes.

Remove the steaks from the pan and let rest for 5 minutes. Meanwhile, make the dressing: Put all the ingredients in a blender and blitz until coarse-fine. Slice the steaks against the grain and divide among the plates. Drizzle the dressing over and serve with the mashed sweet potatoes.

Beef Mole with Chili & Cilantro Cornbread

PREPARATION TIME: 25 minutes, plus making the cornbread | COOKING TIME: 1 hour–1 hour 10 minutes | SERVES: 4

4 tomatoes, quartered
2 onions, quartered
3 garlic cloves, peeled
2 tablespoons olive oil
1 pound 2 ounces
  boneless beef chuck
  or blade steak, cut into
  bite-size pieces
8–10 small shallots,
  peeled
2 dried hot chilies
1 teaspoon ground
  cinnamon
1 teaspoon ground
  coriander
1¼ cups beef stock
1 teaspoon sugar
4 ounces bittersweet
  chocolate, chopped
1 teaspoon dried oregano
juice of 1 lime
kosher salt and freshly
  ground black pepper

TO SERVE
1 large handful of cilantro
  leaves, roughly chopped
1 recipe quantity
  warm Chili & Cilantro
  Cornbread (see
  page 180)
1 lime, quartered

This simple version of beef mole is quite mild, but it's a good introduction to Mexican cooking and I love the richness that the chocolate adds. The cornbread not only tastes divine but is also very quick to make and perfect for mopping up the juices.

Preheat the broiler. Put the tomatoes, onions and garlic cloves in a shallow baking pan and broil, 4–5 inches from the heat, until softened, about 10 minutes. Tip the vegetables into a blender or food processor and blitz until smooth.

While the vegetables are broiling, heat 1 tablespoon of the oil in a frying pan over high heat. Add the beef and cook, stirring occasionally, until well browned all over, 8–10 minutes. A good brown color will add flavor later in the dish.

Heat the remaining tablespoon of oil in a heavy pot or casserole over medium heat. Add the shallots and cook, stirring occasionally, until browned, about 10 minutes. Add the beef to the pot, then add the dried chilies, cinnamon and coriander. Cook for 5 minutes, stirring occasionally, then add the blitzed tomato mixture and the stock. Cover and bring to a boil, then reduce the heat to low and simmer, stirring occasionally, until the meat is tender, 30–40 minutes. Season with salt and pepper, then add the sugar, chocolate, oregano and lime juice. Stir until the chocolate has melted into the sauce.

Serve sprinkled with the cilantro, with some warm chili & cilantro cornbread on the side and lime quarters to squeeze over.

Beef Rendang with Pineapple & Chili Sambal

PREPARATION TIME: 30 minutes, plus making the curry paste and sambal | COOKING TIME: 1 hour | SERVES: 4

1 tablespoon vegetable oil
1¾ pounds rib-eye steak or boneless beef for braising, such as chuck, cut into bite-size pieces
1 recipe quantity Curry Paste (see page 200)
scant 1 cup beef stock
2 tablespoons fish sauce
4 kaffir lime leaves, fresh or dried
1 cinnamon stick
4 lemongrass stalks, tough outer leaves removed and crushed
1 tablespoon light brown sugar or palm sugar
1 small handful of micro cilantro (or cilantro leaves)
kosher salt and freshly ground black pepper

COCONUT RICE
1½ cups Thai jasmine rice
scant ½ cup coconut milk
1 teaspoon yellow mustard seeds

TO SERVE
Pineapple & Chili Sambal (see page 199)

This is an excellent curry: thick, fragrant and rich. It's certainly a world away from your average takeout! The pineapple sambal really adds balance, so do include it.

Heat the oil in a large, heavy casserole over medium-high heat. Add the beef, in batches if necessary, and cook, stirring occasionally, until well browned all over, about 10 minutes. You want a good brown color, because it adds flavor later. Add the curry paste and cook for 5 more minutes, then add the stock, fish sauce, kaffir lime leaves, cinnamon stick and lemongrass. Bring to a boil, then reduce the heat to low and simmer, stirring occasionally, until the beef is tender and the sauce is thick and a rich golden brown, about 40 minutes for rib-eye steak and 1 hour 10 minutes for chuck steak.

Meanwhile, make the coconut rice: Put the rice in a large saucepan with the coconut milk, mustard seeds and a pinch of salt. Add enough water to the pan so that the liquid comes to just under ½ inch above the rice. Cover the pan with a tight-fitting lid and bring to a boil, then reduce the heat to low and simmer until all the liquid has been absorbed and the rice is cooked, 15–20 minutes. Remove from the heat. Fluff up the rice with a fork, then cover the pan again and set aside.

Add the sugar to the rendang and season with salt and pepper. Stir through the cilantro, then serve with the coconut rice and the sambal on the side.

Beef, Bok Choy & Bamboo Shoot Stir-Fry

PREPARATION TIME: 20 minutes | COOKING TIME: 35 minutes | SERVES: 4

heaped 1 cup long-grain white rice, such as Thai jasmine or basmati
1 pound 5 ounces rib-eye steak, trimmed and cut into strips
2 teaspoons cornstarch
3½ tablespoons rice wine or dry sherry
1 tablespoon soy sauce
2 teaspoons vegetable oil
1 teaspoon toasted sesame oil
1-inch piece of fresh gingerroot, peeled and finely chopped
2 garlic cloves, finely chopped
1 hot red chili, seeded and finely diced
1 red bell pepper, seeded and sliced into strips
4 small heads of bok choy, quartered
6 ounces drained, canned bamboo shoots in 1-inch pieces (about 1 cup)
kosher salt and freshly ground black pepper

Stir-fries are so quick and easy. They are a great way to get veggies into your diet and they can be made very tasty with the addition of ginger, garlic and chili. This recipe can be varied by using chicken, pork or shrimp instead of steak.

Tip the rice into a saucepan and add enough water to the pan so that the liquid comes to just under ½ inch above the rice. Cover with a tight-fitting lid and bring to a boil, then reduce the heat to low and simmer until all the water has been absorbed and the rice is cooked, 15–20 minutes. Remove from the heat. Fluff up the rice with a fork, then cover the pan again and set aside.

Put the beef in a bowl and season with salt and pepper. Add the cornstarch and toss until the beef is well coated. Mix the rice wine and soy sauce together in a small bowl.

With all the other stir-fry ingredients prepared and to hand, heat the vegetable oil in a wok or large frying pan until very hot. Stir-fry the beef in the oil until lightly cooked and brown, about 4 minutes, then remove to a plate.

Heat the wok or pan again until very hot, then add the sesame oil, ginger, garlic, chili and all the vegetables. Stir-fry for 8 minutes, then add 1 tablespoon water and the rice wine and soy sauce mix and toss through. Tip the beef and any juices back into the wok and quickly toss until everything is combined and the beef is heated through. Serve immediately, with the rice.

Venison Steaks with Pickled Red Cabbage & Truffle-Polenta Fries

PREPARATION TIME: 20 minutes, plus 20 minutes setting time | COOKING TIME: 1½ hours | SERVES: 4

vegetable oil, for frying
4 venison steaks
kosher salt and freshly
  ground black pepper

PICKLED RED CABBAGE
1 teaspoon juniper berries
1 bay leaf
scant 1 cup red wine
  vinegar
¼ cup packed brown
  sugar
1 small head of red
  cabbage, cored and very
  finely sliced

TRUFFLE-POLENTA FRIES
4 cups vegetable stock
4 tablespoons butter
1⅓ cups instant polenta
1¼ cups grated Parmesan
  cheese
1 tablespoon chopped
  truffle paste
1 teaspoon truffle oil
scant ½ cup olive oil

Venison is not only very high in iron but also a very low-fat source of protein. The polenta fries make a great side dish, but are also good served by themselves as a nibble.

To make the truffle-polenta fries, line a 7- by 10-inch baking pan with plastic wrap. Put the stock and butter in a saucepan and bring to a boil, then quickly pour in the polenta and stir well, removing any lumps. Reduce the heat to low and simmer, stirring continuously, for 15 minutes. Add 1 cup of the Parmesan and season with salt and pepper. Add the truffle paste and oil and mix until well combined, then scrape the mixture into the lined pan. Let cool to room temperature, then refrigerate for 20 minutes to set.

While the polenta is setting, make the pickled red cabbage: Put the juniper berries, bay leaf, vinegar and sugar in a saucepan and bring to a boil. Reduce the heat to low, add the red cabbage and stir well, then cover and simmer, stirring occasionally, until the cabbage is tender, about 40 minutes. Set aside.

When the cabbage is cooked, preheat the oven to 350°F. Unmold the polenta onto a cutting board and cut into sticks ¾ inch wide and 3¼ inches long. Pour the olive oil into a large frying pan and set over medium-high heat. When hot, fry the polenta sticks until golden brown all over, about 5 minutes. Transfer the fries to a baking sheet, sprinkle with the remaining Parmesan and put into the oven to keep hot.

Meanwhile, heat the vegetable oil in another frying pan over medium-high heat. Season the venison steaks with salt and pepper, then put them in the hot pan and cook until browned on the outside but still quite pink in the center, about 6 minutes per side, depending on thickness.

Serve the venison steaks with the truffle-polenta fries and warm pickled red cabbage on the side.

"Venison is my favorite meat. It has a richness and texture that beef can lack."

Fried Sea Bass with Micro Herb & Bell Pepper Salad

PREPARATION TIME: 10 minutes | COOKING TIME: 10 minutes | SERVES: 4

2 carrots, peeled and cut into matchsticks
1 red bell pepper, seeded and finely sliced
3 scallions, finely sliced
4 skin-on sea bass fillets
1 teaspoon vegetable or peanut oil
2 tablespoons soy sauce
1 teaspoon mirin
1 teaspoon toasted sesame oil
1-inch piece of fresh gingerroot, peeled and finely grated
1 small handful of micro cress
1 small handful of micro mizuna
1 small handful of micro cilantro
1 small handful of micro Thai basil
kosher salt and freshly ground black pepper

TO SERVE
1½ cups basmati rice, boiled (optional)

This is a simple dish, but people adore it. It is clean food and great for a detox menu or a weekday dinner with some jasmine rice and steamed bok choy. This is what you want when you've been over-indulging in other parts of your life!

Put the carrots, bell pepper and scallions in a serving bowl and toss together. Using a sharp knife, score the skin on the sea bass and season the fillets on both sides with salt and pepper.

Heat a large frying pan over medium heat. Add the oil and then the sea bass fillets, skin-side down. Cook the fillets until the skin is crisp and golden and the fish is almost cooked through, about 8 minutes. Flip the fillets over and cook for 1 more minute—just enough to set but not color the flesh.

While the sea bass is cooking, mix the soy sauce, mirin, sesame oil and ginger together in a small bowl. Add the micro greens and herbs to the carrot salad and dress with half the soy dressing.

Drizzle the remaining soy dressing over the sea bass and serve with the salad and some basmati rice, if desired.

Pan-Fried Salmon with Anchovy & Lemon Butter & Creamy Champ

PREPARATION TIME: 25 minutes | COOKING TIME: 35 minutes | SERVES: 4

1 pound 2 ounces
  potatoes, peeled and
  cut into chunks
2 tablespoons butter
2 tablespoons heavy
  cream
8 scallions, finely sliced
2 teaspoons olive oil
4 skin-on pieces of
  salmon fillet
9 ounces broccoli rabe or
  broccolini, trimmed
kosher salt and freshly
  ground black pepper

ANCHOVY & LEMON
BUTTER
2 anchovy fillets in oil,
  drained
grated zest of ¼ lemon
5 tablespoons unsalted
  butter, softened
¼ teaspoon lemon juice

The combination of healthy salmon with super-comforting champ is great. The sharp flavors in the anchovy and lemon butter add the perfect balancing touch.

To make the anchovy and lemon butter, blitz the anchovies and lemon zest in a mini blender until finely chopped. Add the butter and lemon juice, then blitz again to a smooth paste. Set aside.

Put the potatoes in a large saucepan, cover with water and bring to a boil. Reduce the heat to low, cover and simmer until cooked, about 20 minutes. Drain the potatoes in a colander and let steam-dry for a few minutes, then return to the pan and mash (use a potato masher or, for a finer texture, pass through a potato ricer). Add the butter, cream and scallions and season generously with salt and pepper. Keep warm.

Heat a frying pan over medium heat. Pour the oil into the hot frying pan, then put the salmon fillets, skin-side down, in the pan. Cook until golden and crisp, about 8 minutes, then flip over and cook for 4 minutes longer.

Meanwhile, cook the broccoli in a saucepan of boiling water until al dente, about 5 minutes. Drain well, then toss with the anchovy and lemon butter.

Serve the salmon with the champ and the broccoli. Drizzle any leftover melted anchovy and lemon butter over the top before serving.

Mussels with Sauternes, Saffron & Micro Cilantro

PREPARATION TIME: 15 minutes | COOKING TIME: 15 minutes | SERVES: 4

4½ pounds mussels
1 tablespoon olive oil
2 large shallots, thinly
   sliced
4 garlic cloves, thinly
   sliced
a pinch of saffron threads
scant ½ cup Sauternes or
   other sweet wine
¼ cup heavy cream
1 tablespoon orange juice
1 large handful of micro
   cilantro

TO SERVE
crusty bread

Sweet sauternes wine and saffron go very well together, and here I have combined them to make a wonderful rich broth in which to cook tender mussels. Use regular cilantro if micro isn't available.

Scrub and clean the mussels in cold water, removing any grit, barnacles and beards. Rinse the mussels again under cold water for several minutes. Discard any muscles that have broken shells or that don't close if they are tapped.

Heat the oil in a large pot over medium-low heat. Add the shallots and garlic and fry, stirring occasionally, until soft and translucent but not browned, about 5 minutes.

Turn the heat up to high and tip in the mussels, saffron and wine. Cover the pot with a tight-fitting lid and cook for 5 minutes. Remove from the heat, pour in the cream and orange juice and season with salt and pepper. Stir or shake the pot to mix. Return the pot to the heat and cook, still covered, for 5 more minutes. Discard any mussels that haven't opened.

Serve in deep bowls with the micro cilantro sprinkled over the top and crusty bread on the side.

Smoked Trout with Micro Cilantro & Coconut Rice

PREPARATION TIME: 20 minutes | COOKING TIME: 45 minutes | SERVES: 4

1½ cups Thai jasmine rice
scant ½ cup coconut milk
1 tablespoon vegetable oil
2 hot red chilies, seeded
 and finely sliced
3 shallots, finely sliced
3 garlic cloves,
 finely chopped
2 scallions, finely sliced
1 tablespoon light soy
 sauce
2 eggs, beaten
1 small handful of
 micro cilantro
 or cilantro leaves
11 ounces skinless
 smoked trout fillet,
 flaked

TO SERVE
1 handful of toasted
 coconut shavings
 (see page 154)
2 limes, cut into wedges

Coconut rice with smoked fish, herbs and specks of chili is quite an unusual combination of flavors—a kind of Thai-style kedgeree. In addition to being unusual, it tastes fantastic!

Tip the rice into a saucepan and pour in the coconut milk. Add enough water so that the liquid comes to just under ½ inch above the rice. Cover with a tight-fitting lid and bring to a boil, then reduce the heat to low and simmer until all the liquid has been absorbed and the rice is cooked, about 20 minutes. Remove from the heat and fluff up the rice with a fork. Set aside, uncovered.

Heat the oil in a wok or frying pan over medium heat. Add the chilies, shallots, garlic and scallions and cook, stirring occasionally, until fragrant and softened, about 8 minutes. Add the coconut rice and soy sauce, mix well and continue cooking until heated through, about 8 more minutes. Make a little space to the side of the pan and add the beaten eggs. Whisk the eggs again lightly and cook until they are lightly set, 2–3 minutes longer.

Add the cilantro and flaked smoked trout and toss all the ingredients together, including the cooked eggs. Cook for a final 5 minutes.

Scatter the toasted coconut shavings over the top and serve, with lime wedges on the side for squeezing over.

Pancetta-Wrapped Halibut with Clams & Celery Shoots

PREPARATION TIME: 10 minutes | COOKING TIME: 20 minutes | SERVES: 4

2 tablespoons butter
4 carrots, peeled and thinly sliced on the diagonal
2 celery sticks, thinly sliced on the diagonal
$2/3$ cup fish, chicken or vegetable stock
4 pieces of skinless halibut or cod fillets
8 thin strips of pancetta
1 tablespoon olive oil
14 ounces small hardshell clams, washed under cold water
$1/4$ cup white wine
3 ounces celery shoots (microgreen)

TO SERVE
crusty bread (optional)

Halibut is great when wrapped in savory pancetta. Here I have also braised some carrots and celery and added some lightly cooked clams. Serve this with crusty bread to soak up the flavors.

Heat the butter in a saucepan over medium heat. Add the carrots and celery and stir until well coated with butter. Add the stock and bring to a boil, then lower the heat and simmer, uncovered, for 20 minutes.

Meanwhile, cook the halibut and clams: Wrap each halibut fillet in two strips of pancetta, keeping the seams on one side of the fish. Heat the oil in a large, deep frying pan over medium heat. Put the halibut in the pan and cook until the pancetta is golden brown and the flesh of the fish is milky-colored in the center, about 4 minutes per side. Remove the fillets from the pan and cover with foil to keep warm.

Turn the heat up and add the clams and wine. Cover the pan with a tight-fitting lid and cook until the clams have opened, about 5 minutes. Discard any clams that remain closed.

Serve the halibut fillets with the carrot and celery mixture and the clams. Sprinkle with celery shoots and serve with crusty bread, if desired.

“Halibut is the king of fish with its wonderful close-textured flesh.”

Soba Noodles with Crab & Micro Shiso Cress

PREPARATION TIME: 20 minutes | COOKING TIME: 10 minutes | SERVES: 4

7 ounces soba noodles
1 teaspoon toasted
   sesame oil
1 teaspoon sesame seeds
1 tablespoon soy sauce,
   plus extra for dressing
   the salad
a pinch of hot chili
   powder
7 ounces cooked
   crabmeat, flaked
   (about 1²/₃ cups)
2 sheets nori seaweed,
   cut into strips with
   scissors
3 scallions, finely sliced
scant 4 ounces pickled
   pink ginger, finely
   chopped
1 tablespoon bonito flakes
   (optional)
1 small handful of micro
   shiso cress

Soba noodles are made with buckwheat flour, which is easier for people with a wheat intolerence to digest. This is a classic Japanese dish, served cold with all the various condiments. I love it because it's super quick to make and very healthy.

Bring a large saucepan of water to a rapid boil, then drop in the soba noodles, separating them as you do so and stirring well to ensure they stay apart. Cook for 7–8 minutes or according to the package directions. Drain the noodles in a colander and rinse under cold water until all the starch and gluten come out and the water runs clear. Tip into a bowl and toss with the sesame oil to prevent the noodles from sticking together.

Mix together the sesame seeds, soy sauce and chili powder in a small bowl. Add to the noodles and toss until well combined. Cover with plastic wrap and refrigerate while you prepare the rest of the accompaniments.

Serve the noodles on a large plate with the crabmeat on top. Put the nori, scallions, pickled ginger and bonito flakes, if using, around the edge. Dress the micro shiso cress with a little soy sauce and scatter over. Serve immediately.

Crab & Saffron Risotto

PREPARATION TIME: 20 minutes | COOKING TIME: 40 minutes | SERVES: 4

3¼ cups fish stock
1 tablespoon olive oil
1 onion, finely diced
2 garlic cloves, finely
  chopped
heaped 1 cup risotto rice,
  such as Arborio
scant ½ cup white wine
a large pinch of saffron
  threads
8 scallions, finely sliced
14 ounces cooked
  crabmeat, flaked
  (about 3 cups)
4 tablespoons butter
1 tablespoon chopped
  flat-leaf parsley
grated zest of 1 lemon,
  or to taste

Many people seem to think that risottos are hard to make, but they just need a little love and attention. Keep stirring them to release the starch in the grains and don't overcook the rice. When you master the art of risottos, you can then experiment with all sorts of flavors.

Put the stock in a saucepan and bring to a boil. Heat the oil in a deep frying pan over medium heat, add the onion and garlic, and cook until softened and translucent, about 5 minutes.

Add the rice and stir to coat with the oil. Pour in the wine and stir until it is all absorbed, then add a ladleful of the hot stock and stir until it is fully absorbed by the rice. Add the saffron, then continue to add the stock, ladleful by ladleful, stirring the rice after each addition, until all the stock is absorbed. This should take about 20 minutes.

Add the scallions and cook for 5 minutes longer, stirring continuously, then add the crabmeat and butter and stir until smooth and creamy. Check the rice: you want it to be tender but still with a little firm bite. Add more stock if it needs further cooking.

Stir in the parsley and lemon zest to taste. Remove the pan from the heat and let the risotto sit for 5 minutes before serving.

Shrimp, Pea Shoot & Lemon Linguine

PREPARATION TIME: 15 minutes | COOKING TIME: 25 minutes | SERVES: 4

14 ounces linguine
2 tablespoons olive oil,
    plus extra for drizzling
14 ounces peeled raw
    tiger shrimp or large
    shrimp, deveined
1 hot red chili, seeded and
    finely chopped
grated zest and juice of
    1 lemon
1 ounce pea shoots
1 small handful of
    flat-leaf parsley
    leaves, chopped
kosher salt and freshly
    ground black pepper

This light, fresh pasta dish is perfect for lunch. You can replace the shrimp with crabmeat or have a vegetarian version with just peas and pea shoots. Adding the pasta along with a little cooking liquid to the shrimp, then cooking a bit more, is the true Italian way.

Bring a large saucepan of lightly salted water to a boil. When boiling rapidly, add the linguine and cook according to the package directions, until al dente.

About halfway through the pasta cooking time, heat the oil in a frying pan over medium heat. Add the shrimp and stir-fry for 4 minutes, then add the chili and continue cooking until the shrimp have turned pink and are cooked through, about 4 minutes longer.

Drain the pasta, keeping a tablespoon of cooking water, and add to the shrimp pan, along with the reserved cooking water, lemon zest and juice, pea shoots and parsley. Stir-fry until all the ingredients are well mixed and the pasta is heated through, 1–2 minutes. Finally, add a generous drizzle of olive oil and season with salt and pepper. Serve immediately.

Pan-Grilled Tuna with Caponata & Basil

PREPARATION TIME: 20 minutes, plus making the mash | COOKING TIME: 1 hour | SERVES: 4

heaped 1/3 cup pine nuts
2 tablespoons olive oil,
    plus extra for frying
1 onion, chopped
3 garlic cloves, finely
    chopped
2 celery sticks, cut into
    1/2-inch cubes
1 red bell pepper, seeded
    and cut into 1/2-inch
    cubes
2 zucchini, cut into
    1/2-inch cubes
1 eggplant, cut into
    1/2-inch cubes
14 ounces canned
    crushed tomatoes
5 teaspoons balsamic
    vinegar
1/4 cup sugar
4 tuna steaks, weighing
    6–7 ounces each
1 large handful of basil
kosher salt and freshly
    ground black pepper

TO SERVE
Roasted Garlic & Olive-Oil
    Mash (see page 204)

Caponata is a southern Italian, slightly sweet and sour vegetable stew, very similar to ratatouille. It's also great served cold with cold cuts and cheese.

Heat a frying pan over medium-high heat. Add the pine nuts and toast until fragrant and starting to brown. Tip the pine nuts onto a plate and set aside.

Heat 1 tablespoon of the oil in a large saucepan over medium heat. Add the onion, garlic and celery and fry, stirring occasionally, until softened and translucent, about 10 minutes. Season with salt and pepper, then add the bell pepper and zucchini and stir to mix. Continue cooking gently.

Meanwhile, heat the remaining tablespoon of oil in the frying pan over very high heat. Add the eggplant cubes, in batches, and fry, stirring occasionally, until slightly colored, about 5 minutes.

Add the eggplant to the zucchini and pepper mixture along with the tomatoes. Bring to a boil, then reduce the heat to low and simmer until thick, 30–40 minutes. Add the balsamic vinegar and sugar and check the seasoning, then add the toasted pine nuts. Keep warm.

Heat a ridged grill pan over high heat until smoking hot. Lightly oil both sides of the tuna steaks and season with salt and pepper. Add the tuna to the pan and pan-grill until well seared but still pink in the middle, 3–4 minutes per side. Adjust the cooking time according to the thickness of the steaks and the desired degree of doneness.

Spoon the caponata over the tuna steaks, sprinkle with micro basil and serve with Roasted Garlic & Olive-Oil Mash.

Pad Thai

PREPARATION TIME: 20 minutes | COOKING TIME: 15 minutes | SERVES: 4

9 ounces rice stick
noodles
1 tablespoon peanut oil,
plus extra for dressing
2 tablespoons dried
shrimp
2 shallots, sliced
3 garlic cloves, finely
chopped
6 ounces peeled and
deveined raw tiger
shrimp or large shrimp
4 ounces fried tofu,
cut into cubes or strips
2 eggs, beaten
1½ cups bean sprouts
4 scallions or Chinese
chives, roughly sliced
1 small handful of
cilantro leaves

PAD THAI SAUCE
1 teaspoon hot chili
powder
1 tablespoon fish sauce
1 tablespoon light soy
sauce
1 tablespoon tamarind
water
1 tablespoon sugar

TO SERVE
⅓ cup finely chopped
peanuts
2 limes, cut into wedges

This is a classic dish that gets completely destroyed by takeouts all over the world. It is quite sophisticated, and does need some delicate balancing. Practice your Pad Thai sauce and personalize it to your tastes, adding more chili for heat, more tamarind for sour and more sugar for sweetness. A brilliant dish.

To make the sauce, whisk all the ingredients together in a small bowl until well combined. Set aside.

Put the rice sticks in a heatproof bowl, cover with boiling water and let soak for 10 minutes. Drain the noodles in a colander and rinse under cold water. Return the noodles to the bowl and dress with a little oil to prevent them from sticking together. Meanwhile, put the dried shrimp in another bowl, cover with hot water and soak for 5 minutes, then drain.

Heat the oil in a wok or large frying pan over medium heat. Add the shallots, garlic, soaked dried shrimp and tiger shrimp and stir-fry for 5 minutes. Add the tofu, soaked noodles and prepared sauce and cook for 8 minutes longer, stirring occasionally. Make a little space to the side of the pan and add the beaten eggs. Beat the eggs again lightly and cook until they are just set, 2–3 minutes. Finally, add the bean sprouts, scallions and cilantro and toss all the ingredients together, including the cooked eggs, until combined.

Serve sprinkled with the chopped peanuts, with lime wedges on the side.

Pan-Grilled Shrimp with Mango

PREPARATION TIME: 15 minutes | COOKING TIME: 8 minutes | SERVES: 4

1 hot red chili, seeded and finely chopped
2 garlic cloves, minced
1 tablespoon olive oil
1 pound 2 ounces raw tiger shrimp or large shrimp, peeled and deveined
2 ripe mangoes
1 head of baby romaine, leaves separated
kosher salt and freshly ground black pepper

TO SERVE
juice of 1 lime
1 small handful of micro cilantro

This is a really easy salad and is very delicious, despite its simplicity. The flavors are clean and vibrant. If I can find good quality crabmeat or even lobster, I use that too.

Whisk together the chili, garlic and olive oil in a large bowl, then add the shrimp and toss well.

Using a sharp knife, carefully slice each mango down either side of the pit. Peel the skin off the mango sides, then cut the flesh into slices. Peel the remaining parts of the mango and slice the flesh from the pit. Set aside.

Heat a ridged grill pan until very hot. Add the shrimp, season with salt and pepper and pan-grill until they have turned pink and are cooked through, about 4 minutes per side.

To serve, arrange the mango slices on the lettuce, then top with the shrimp. Squeeze the lime juice over and sprinkle with the micro cilantro.

Summer Vegetable & Truffle-Oil Pizzas

PREPARATION TIME: 20 minutes, plus making the pizza dough | COOKING TIME: 45 minutes | SERVES: 4

4 zucchini
2 teaspoons olive oil
9 ounces drained, canned or jarred artichoke hearts, halved
7 ounces drained, jarred roasted red bell peppers, cut into strips (about 1 cup)
1 recipe quantity Pizza Dough, formed into 4 pizza bases (see page 204)
truffle oil, for drizzling
1½ cups grated Parmesan cheese
4 ounces micro basil, micro mizuna or a combination of both

CARAMELIZED SHALLOT PURÉE
4 tablespoons butter
8 large shallots, sliced
1 thyme sprig, leaves picked
1 teaspoon sugar
4 teaspoons heavy cream
kosher salt and freshly ground black pepper

This variation on a pizza was inspired by a trip to the French Riviera. I have kept the traditional thin crust, but then made a caramelized shallot purée instead of a tomato base. This is topped with summery veggies, Parmesan cheese and a drizzle of truffle oil to create a deluxe, seriously delicious pizza.

To make the caramelized shallot purée, melt the butter in a frying pan over medium-low heat. Add the shallots and thyme and cook gently until the shallots are softened and translucent, about 20 minutes. Add the sugar and cream, cover and cook until caramelized, about 15 minutes longer. Season with salt and pepper. Transfer the mixture to a food processor or blender and blitz to a fine purée. If the mixture looks too thin for a good pizza base topping, return it to the pan and cook very gently, stirring occasionally, until the excess liquid has evaporated.

Preheat the oven to 400°F and put two baking sheets in the oven to heat.

Slice the zucchini lengthwise into thin ribbons using a swivel-bladed vegetable peeler. Combine in a bowl with the olive oil, artichoke hearts and roasted pepper strips and toss together.

Fork the pizza bases all over, then put them on the hot baking sheets. Spread the caramelized shallot purée evenly over the bases, then arrange the dressed vegetables on top. Put the pizzas in the oven and bake until cooked and golden, 8–10 minutes. Remove from the oven, drizzle some truffle oil over and sprinkle with the Parmesan and micro herbs. Serve immediately.

Spelt's nutty, earthy undertones and chewy texture work very well in risottos."

Spelt & Roasted Butternut Squash Risotto

PREPARATION TIME: 15 minutes | COOKING TIME: 1 hour | SERVES: 4

3 cups peeled, seeded and diced butternut squash (about 12 ounces)
2 tablespoons olive oil
4 cups vegetable stock
1 onion, finely diced
2 garlic cloves, finely chopped
7 ounces spelt berries (about 1 heaped cup)
scant ½ cup white wine
1 tablespoon chopped sage leaves
2 tablespoons butter
½ cup grated Parmesan cheese
kosher salt and freshly ground black pepper

TO SERVE
1 ounce small arugula leaves
3 tablespoons pumpkin seeds
balsamic vinegar

I have used butternut squash and sage for the flavorings in this hearty risotto, but wild mushrooms, chicken, asparagus and Jerusalem artichokes would all work well, too.

Preheat the oven to 400°F. Put the butternut squash in a shallow baking pan, drizzle 1 tablespoon of the oil over and season with salt and pepper. Roast until tender, about 15 minutes.

Meanwhile, put the stock in a saucepan and bring to a boil, then reduce to a simmer. At the same time, heat the remaining tablespoon of oil in a deep wide pan over medium heat, add the onion and garlic and cook until softened and translucent, about 5 minutes. Add the spelt berries and stir to coat with the oil.

Pour in the wine and stir until it is all absorbed, then add a ladleful of the hot stock and stir until it is fully absorbed by the spelt. Continue to add the stock, ladleful by ladleful, stirring the spelt to absorb the stock after each addition. Adding the stock slowly should take 30–40 minutes in total. About 20 minutes into the spelt cooking time, add the butternut squash and sage.

During the latter part of the cooking process, check the spelt regularly. You want it to be cooked but still with a little firmness, and you may not need all the stock. When it is just about the desired consistency, add the butter and Parmesan and season with salt and pepper.

Serve the risotto with the arugula leaves and pumpkin seeds sprinkled over the top and a generous drizzle of balsamic vinegar.

Herb & Ricotta Ravioli with Buttered Rainbow Chard

PREPARATION TIME: 20 minutes, plus 30 minutes resting time and making the dough | COOKING TIME: 10 minutes | SERVES: 4

14 ounces ricotta cheese
   (about 1¾ cups)
1 small handful of basil
1 small handful of mint
a pinch of freshly grated
   nutmeg
1 recipe quantity Pasta
   Dough (see page 203),
   rolled into 2 sheets
1 egg yolk, beaten
semolina, for dusting
4 tablespoons butter
2 ounces rainbow chard,
   stalks and leaves
   separated
kosher salt and freshly
   ground black pepper

TO SERVE
grated Parmesan cheese

Making your own pasta is a great habit to form. It is much easier than you'd think and the results are very satisfying. These are delicate herb raviolis with chard, but you can make many variations. My other favorite is squash and amaretti with sage brown butter.

Put the ricotta, herbs and nutmeg in a blender or food processor and blitz until smooth. Tip the ricotta mixture into a bowl and season with salt and pepper, then cover with plastic wrap and refrigerate for 30 minutes.

Lay one pasta dough sheet on a large cutting board. Put individual heaped teaspoonfuls of the ricotta filling all over the sheet at 1¼-inch intervals. Brush around the filling with the beaten egg yolk, then put the second sheet of pasta over the top. Carefully press down around the filling mounds to seal the sheets together, then, using a sharp knife or a ravioli cutter, cut into squares. Put the ravioli on a tray dusted with semolina.

Bring a large pot of lightly salted water to a boil. When boiling rapidly, add the ravioli and cook until al dente, about 8 minutes.

Meanwhile, melt the butter in a large frying pan over medium-low heat. Add the rainbow chard stalks and cook for 2–3 minutes, then add the leaves and cook until wilted and tender, 1–2 minutes.

When the pasta is cooked, drain in a colander, then gently toss with the buttered chard in the pan. Season with salt and pepper and serve immediately, with plenty of grated Parmesan to sprinkle on top.

"Gnocchi should be light little pillows that melt in the mouth."

Potato Gnocchi with Pea-Shoot Pesto & Pecorino Shavings

PREPARATION TIME: 15 minutes | COOKING TIME: 1¼ hours | SERVES: 4

2¼ pounds floury baking
   potatoes, scrubbed
1 egg, beaten
2 cups all-purpose flour
4 tablespoons butter
kosher salt and freshly
   ground black pepper

PEA-SHOOT PESTO
6 ounces Pecorino Sardo
   cheese
6 ounces pea shoots
1 small handful of basil
2 garlic cloves, peeled
heaped ⅓ cup pine nuts
⅔ cup olive oil

I started making gnocchi when I was in Sardinia, where I fell in love with the region's Pecorino Sardo, which is a smooth, slightly salty hard cheese that is fantastic in pesto. Gnocchi should have a light texture, so do not add too much flour, as this will make them heavy.

Preheat the oven to 400°F. Prick the potatoes, then bake until cooked through, about 1 hour.

Meanwhile, make the pesto: Set aside about one-third of the Pecorino cheese and put the remainder in a blender or food processor with the rest of the pesto ingredients. Blitz to a rough paste. Season with salt and pepper and set aside. Using a swivel-bladed vegetable peeler, slice the remaining Pecorino into shavings. Set aside.

Remove the potatoes from the oven, cut them in half and scoop out the flesh into a bowl. Keeping the potato in the bowl covered with a kitchen towel so it doesn't dry out and go hard, gradually press it through a potato ricer or a food mill into another large bowl. Add the egg and flour to the riced potato and mix into a soft dough. Be careful not to overwork the dough, or it will become gluey and tough.

Bring a large pot of lightly salted water to a rapid boil. Roll the dough on a lightly floured surface into sausage shapes roughly 1 inch wide and 15 inches long. Cut into 1-inch-long pieces and lay these gnocchi on a floured plate. Add half the gnocchi to the saucepan of boiling water and cook for 5 minutes, then remove with a slotted spoon and drain. Repeat with the remaining gnocchi.

Melt the butter in a frying pan over medium heat. Add the gnocchi to the pan, season with salt and pepper and fry, turning over occasionally, until lightly colored, about 5 minutes. Add the pesto and mix until the gnocchi is well coated. Serve immediately, sprinkled with the Pecorino shavings.

Broccolini & Sweet Potato Tempura

PREPARATION TIME: 20 minutes, plus making the sauce and noodles | COOKING TIME: 35 minutes | SERVES: 4

2 cups vegetable oil
7 ounces broccolini, trimmed
2 sweet potatoes, thinly sliced

DAIKON & CARROT SALAD
2 ounces daikon, peeled and cut into matchsticks
2 ounces carrot, peeled and cut into matchsticks
1 teaspoon sesame seeds
1 tablespoon soy sauce

TEMPURA BATTER
6 tablespoons cornstarch
1½ cups all-purpose flour
1¼ cups soda water, very cold
kosher salt and freshly ground black pepper

TO SERVE
Dipping Sauce (see page 198), for serving
Crab & Micro Shiso Cress (see page 123) (optional)

The secret to my tempura is to use cornstarch and soda water for extra bubbles of air, making a super-light batter. I have used broccolini and sweet potato for contrasting colors. This batter and sauce also go well with tiger shrimp, white fish and calamari.

To make the salad, toss together the daikon, carrot, sesame seeds and soy sauce in a small bowl until well combined, then set aside.

Preheat the oven to 275°F and put a baking sheet in the oven to heat up.

Heat the oil in a large, deep saucepan over medium heat. It will be hot enough for deep-frying when a piece of vegetable dropped into the oil sizzles immediately. When the oil is hot, make the tempura batter by whisking the cornstarch, flour and soda water together in a large bowl until smooth; season with salt and pepper. (You need to make the batter at the last minute so that the bubbles aren't lost.)

One piece at a time, dip the broccolini and sweet potato pieces in the batter, then carefully drop into the hot oil and deep-fry until a light golden brown, 6–8 minutes. Don't put too many pieces in the oil at the same time, or the temperature of the oil will drop. As the tempura vegetables are fried, scoop out with a slotted spoon, drain on paper towels and transfer to the heated baking sheet to keep warm.

Serve the tempura with the daikon and carrot salad and dipping sauce on the side, and with Crab & Micro Shiso Cress, if desired.

Desserts
& Cheese

White Chocolate & Ginger Cream with Passion-Fruit Curd

PREPARATION TIME: 15 minutes, plus 15 minutes cooling time and 2 hours setting time | COOKING TIME: 10 minutes | SERVES: 4

1¼ cups heavy cream
1 pound 2 ounces white chocolate, finely chopped, plus shavings for decoration
2 teaspoons chopped candied ginger

PASSION-FRUIT CURD
8 passion fruits
½ cup sugar
2 eggs, plus 2 egg yolks
2 tablespoons unsalted butter

White chocolate and ginger are great partners, and make an unusual dessert when topped with a passion-fruit curd. The curd will keep in the refrigerator for about a week and is also amazing served on pancakes, toast and crumpets.

To make the passion-fruit curd, halve the passion fruits and scoop out the flesh and seeds into a saucepan. Add the sugar, eggs and egg yolks and whisk until well combined, then set the saucepan over medium-low heat and stir slowly until the egg mixture thickens, just a few minutes. Do not let it boil.

Add the butter and stir quickly until it melts and the ingredients are well combined. Remove from the heat and let cool to room temperature, then cover with plastic wrap and refrigerate for 1 hour.

Meanwhile, make the chocolate and ginger cream: Heat the cream in a small saucepan over medium heat until it just begins to boil. Remove from the heat and stir in the chocolate. When melted and well combined, add the ginger.

Divide the chocolate mixture among four glass serving dishes, leaving a minimum gap of ½ inch at the top. Refrigerate until set, at least 2 hours. Top with the passion-fruit curd in an even layer and decorate with white chocolate shavings before serving.

Chocolate Fondants with Mint Ice Cream

PREPARATION TIME: 20 minutes, plus 30 minutes infusing time, 30 minutes chilling time, 40 minutes churning time and 1 hour freezing time | COOKING TIME: 15 minutes | SERVES: 4

5 ounces bittersweet chocolate with 70% cacao, chopped

10 tablespoons (1 stick + 2 tablespoons) unsalted butter, plus extra for greasing

3 eggs, plus 3 egg yolks

¾ cup sugar

1 teaspoon salt

scant 1 cup all-purpose flour

2 tablespoons unsweetened cocoa powder, plus extra for the dishes

MINT ICE CREAM

2 cups heavy cream

1 cup whole milk

3 large handfuls of mint leaves

5 egg yolks

¾ cup sugar

To make the ice cream, pour the cream and milk into a saucepan and bring to a boil slowly, stirring continuously. Add two handfuls of mint leaves, reduce the heat to low and simmer for 5 minutes. Remove from the heat and let infuse for 30 minutes. Strain the mixture into a clean saucepan.

Whisk together the 5 egg yolks and sugar in a large bowl until well combined but not bubbly. Bring the mint-flavored cream to a boil over medium heat, then pour it into the yolk mixture, whisking continuously so that the eggs do not cook. Pour the mixture back into the saucepan and heat very gently, stirring continuously, until thickened. Pour the custard into a bowl and let cool, then refrigerate for 30 minutes to chill.

Stir the remaining mint leaves into the chilled custard and pour into an ice-cream machine. Churn according to the manufacturer's directions, then transfer to a freezer container, cover and freeze. (If you don't have an ice-cream machine, refer to the directions for still-freezing on page 161.)

To make the fondants, preheat the oven to 350°F. Grease four 4-ounce ramekins or other individual baking dishes and dust with cocoa powder. Put the chocolate and butter in a heatproof bowl and set it over a saucepan of gently simmering water, making sure the base of the bowl does not touch the water. Heat, stirring occasionally, until the chocolate and butter have melted. Remove the bowl from the pan of water.

Combine the eggs, egg yolks, sugar and salt in a bowl and beat until pale and slightly thickened. Sift the flour and cocoa powder together. Mix the melted chocolate mixture into the egg mixture, then fold in the sifted flour and cocoa. Spoon the mixture into the prepared ramekins and bake until just set, about 8 minutes. Meanwhile, remove the ice cream from the freezer to soften slightly. Serve the chocolate fondants immediately, each topped with a large scoop of mint ice cream.

Cinnamon Lebanese Pudding with Almonds & Pistachios

PREPARATION TIME: 15 minutes, plus 24 hours soaking time and 2 hours chilling time | COOKING TIME: 50 minutes | SERVES: 4

½ cup unblanched almonds
½ cup shelled pistachio nuts
1 cup spring water
¾ cup ground rice
½ cup sugar
½ tablespoon ground caraway
2½ teaspoons ground cinnamon
1¼ teaspoons ground aniseed
½ tablespoon dried shredded coconut
edible gold leaf (optional)

This dessert is called *meghli* in Lebanon, where it is served when a baby is born. It is a rich, highly spiced, ground rice pudding and I have topped it with soaked almonds, pistachios and gold leaf. When you soak nuts, they sprout and become nutrient-dense.

Put the almonds and pistachios in a large bowl and pour the spring water over. Let soak for 24 hours at room temperature, then drain and rinse. Put the soaked nuts in an airtight container and refrigerate.

Pour 6 cups water into a large saucepan and bring to a boil. Add the ground rice, sugar and spices and stir well, then bring back to a boil. Simmer, stirring occasionally, until the mixture is very thick, about 45 minutes.

Spoon the rice pudding into four 5-ounce glass bowls or pretty pots. Cover with plastic wrap, pressing it onto the surface of the rice pudding so that a skin cannot form, then refrigerate for 2 hours to chill.

Top the puddings with a mixture of soaked almonds and pistachios, then sprinkle with the coconut and decorate with pieces of gold leaf, if desired, before serving. Any leftover nuts can be kept in the refrigerator for snacking.

Greek Rhubarb & Custard Phyllo Pie

PREPARATION TIME: 25 minutes | COOKING TIME: 1 hour 10 minutes | MAKES: 6 squares or 12 triangles

8 sticks of rhubarb,
   trimmed
½ cup sugar
7 tablespoons unsalted
   butter, melted, plus
   extra for greasing
10 sheets of phyllo pastry

CUSTARD FILLING
1½ cups milk
2 teaspoons vanilla
   extract
heaped ¼ cup semolina
   (farina)
½ cup sugar
2 eggs, beaten

SYRUP
½ cup sugar
1 tablespoon honey
1 teaspoon lemon juice

This phyllo pie, which is called *galaktoboureko* in Greek, is equally good without the rhubarb if that isn't in season. Instead you could make it with extra custard filling, and perhaps add some orange-flower water to the syrup.

Preheat the oven to 400°F and lightly grease a baking pan with butter. Cut the rhubarb into 8-inch lengths and spread in the pan along with any shorter pieces. Sprinkle the sugar over and bake for 15 minutes. Remove from the oven, leaving the oven on.

Meanwhile, to make the custard filling, put the milk, vanilla, semolina, sugar and eggs in a heavy-based saucepan set over medium-low heat. Stirring constantly, heat slowly until thickened, without letting the mixture boil. This will take about 15 minutes. Remove from the heat and let cool.

Lay a sheet of phyllo pastry on the work surface and brush it with some of the melted butter. Put a second sheet on top and brush with butter. Repeat with two more sheets of phyllo. Line an 8-inch square baking dish with the buttered layered phyllo, pressing it into the corners. Spread the rhubarb on top, then pour the custard over. Butter the remaining six sheets of phyllo, layering them as you go. Put the phyllo on top of the custard and tuck in all around the edges.

Using a sharp knife, cut the phyllo pie into six squares, then cut each square into two triangles, if desired. Bake until the pastry is crisp and golden, about 40 minutes.

Meanwhile, to make the syrup, put all the ingredients in a saucepan and add scant ½ cup water. Bring to a boil, then reduce the heat to low and simmer, stirring continuously, until the sugar dissolves. Set aside.

Remove the baking dish from the oven, pour the syrup over the phyllo pie and let cool slightly. Serve warm.

Milk Chocolate & Sea-Salt Caramel Pots

PREPARATION TIME: 15 minutes, plus 3 hours setting time | COOKING TIME: 10 minutes | SERVES: 4

SEA-SALT CARAMEL
1 cup sugar
scant ¾ cup heavy cream
a large pinch of sea-salt
  crystals
1 egg yolk

MILK-CHOCOLATE CREAM
1¼ cups heavy cream
1 teaspoon vanilla extract
11 ounces milk chocolate,
  finely chopped
2 egg yolks

CARAMEL SHARDS
1½ cups sugar
1 tablespoon sea salt
  crystals

To make the sea-salt caramel, stir the sugar and about 1 tablespoon water in a saucepan over high heat until melted, then bring to a boil. Reduce the heat to low and simmer until the sugar starts to caramelize and turn golden. Watch closely because the sugar can turn too dark very quickly. Also, try not to get any sugar crystals on the side of the pan, because they will cause the caramel to crystallize.

Remove from the heat. Add the cream and salt and mix until well combined. The cream will bubble and the caramelized sugar may start to harden. If this happens, return the pan to low heat and stir constantly until the sugar melts again and the mixture is smooth. Remove from the heat and let cool slightly, then whisk in the egg yolk. Pour the caramel into four 5-ounce serving glasses or ramekins and refrigerate for 1 hour to set.

To make the milk-chocolate cream, put the cream and vanilla in a saucepan over medium-high heat and bring just to a boil, then remove from the heat and add the chocolate. Stir until completely melted, then let cool for 5 minutes before whisking in the egg yolks. Remove the ramekins from the refrigerator and pour the chocolate cream over the top of the sea-salt caramel. Return to the refrigerator to set for 1–2 hours.

To make the caramel shards, line a baking sheet with parchment paper. Using the sugar and scant ¼ cup water, follow the method above for caramelizing the sugar. Pour immediately onto the prepared baking sheet, sprinkle the sea salt crystals over the top and let cool and harden.

To serve, break the sheet of caramel into shards and use to decorate the caramel pots.

Pomegranate Panna Cottas with Red-Currant & Orange Salad

PREPARATION TIME: 20 minutes, plus 3 hours setting time or overnight | COOKING TIME: 3 minutes | SERVES: 4

6 gelatin sheets
2/3 cup heavy cream
2/3 cup milk
1¼ cups pomegranate juice
3 tablespoons grenadine syrup
¼ cup sugar

RED-CURRANT & ORANGE SALAD
2 oranges
7 ounces red currants (about 1½ cups)

It's probably obvious by now that pomegranate is one of my favorite ingredients! These pink, wobbly panna cottas are a little different from the usual dessert.

Soak the gelatin sheets in a small bowl of cold water until softened, about 5 minutes. Meanwhile, put the cream, milk, pomegranate juice, grenadine and sugar in a saucepan over medium-high heat and bring to just below boiling point. Remove from the heat. Squeeze the gelatin sheets to remove excess water, then stir into the pomegranate mixture until melted.

Pour into four individual 7-ounce metal molds; or, if you don't want to unmold the panna cottas onto dessert plates, pour the mixture into four pretty serving bowls. Refrigerate for at least 3 hours, or overnight, to set.

One hour before serving, make the red-currant and orange salad: Using a sharp knife, peel the oranges, removing all the skin and pith, then carefully cut out the sections.

If the panna cottas are in metal molds, quickly dip them into a bowl of very hot water, then upturn on dessert plates and lift off the molds. Arrange the red currants and orange on top and around the panna cottas. If the panna cottas are in serving bowls, pile the fruit salad into the middle of the bowls and serve.

"Beautiful and delicious, these fruity panna cottas make a great end to a meal."

Caramelized Coconut-Rice Pudding

PREPARATION TIME: 15 minutes | COOKING TIME: 1 hour 10 minutes | SERVES: 4

2 tablespoons unsalted
    butter
¼ cup packed light
    brown sugar
½ cup short-grain rice
1¾ cups coconut milk
1 cup milk
4 teaspoons Malibu
    rum liqueur
1 small coconut

TO SERVE
lime wedges

This dessert was inspired by my time in Asia. The caramelized, almost palm-sugar-like flavor mixed with the rich coconut rice is soothing and comforting. It makes a great finale to a spicy feast.

Preheat the oven to 320°F. Melt the butter in a large, ovenproof pan over medium-low heat, then add the sugar and cook until melted, caramelized and bubbling, 5–8 minutes. Stir in the rice, coconut milk, milk and Malibu. The mixture may clump up and stick together at this point, but don't worry.

Cover the pan with a tight-fitting lid (or line with foil and then set the lid on top) and transfer to the oven to bake for 30 minutes. Remove from the oven and stir well, then return to the oven to bake until the rice is cooked through and the sauce is thick and creamy, about 30 minutes longer.

Toward the end of the cooking time, pierce the "eyes" at the top of the coconut and drain out the liquid, then crack the coconut in half with a meat mallet, rolling pin or hammer. Using a swivel-bladed vegetable peeler, slice shavings of coconut and spread on a baking sheet.

Remove the rice pudding from the oven and keep hot. Turn on the broiler. Slide the baking sheet under the broiler and toast the coconut shavings for a few minutes until golden brown.

Sprinkle the toasted coconut shavings over the top of the rice pudding and serve, with lime wedges on the side for squeezing over. Store any leftover coconut shavings in an airtight container in a cool place for up to 3 weeks—they are also great for decorating the Coconut & Lime Cake on page 189.

Cassia-Scented Custard Tart with Apple Compote

PREPARATION TIME: 20 minutes, plus making the pastry | COOKING TIME: 1½ hours | SERVES: 8

1 recipe quantity Sweet
   Pastry dough (see
   page 202)
1 vanilla bean
3 cups heavy cream
2 (2-inch) pieces of
   cassia bark
¾ cup sugar
4 eggs, plus 4 egg yolks,
   reserving a little egg
   white for brushing
1 teaspoon ground
   cinnamon

APPLE COMPOTE
4 crisp green apples,
   such as Granny Smith,
   peeled, cored and
   thickly sliced
⅔ cup golden raisins
1 teaspoon lemon juice
¼ cup sugar

Preheat the oven to 350°F. Roll out the pastry on a lightly floured surface until about ⅛ inch thick and large enough to line a 10-inch tart pan with a ¾-inch overhang. Carefully lift the pastry into the pan and press into the flutes; the pastry should rise slightly above the rim of the pan. Line the pastry shell with parchment paper and weight down with dried beans or rice.

Bake for 20 minutes, then remove the parchment paper and weights. Prick the bottom of the pastry shell with a fork and brush with beaten egg white. Return to the oven to bake until just starting to turn golden, about 5 minutes. Remove from the oven and set aside. Reduce the oven temperature to 275°F.

While the pastry shell is baking, use a sharp knife to split the vanilla bean in half and scrape the seeds into a saucepan with the cream and cassia bark. Bring slowly to a boil. Reduce the heat and simmer gently for 4 minutes.

Meanwhile, beat the sugar, eggs and egg yolks together in a bowl until light and fluffy. When the cream is ready, slowly pour it into the bowl, beating until well combined. Pour the mixture through a fine strainer into another bowl or pitcher, removing the cassia bark and any lumps, then pour the mixture into the pastry shell in an even layer. Sprinkle with the cinnamon. Bake the tart until just set but still quite wobbly, 30–40 minutes. Let cool before trimming the pastry to the height of the tin using a sharp knife.

To make the apple compote, put the apples, raisins, lemon juice and sugar in a saucepan over medium-high heat. Bring to a boil, then reduce the heat to low and simmer for 10 minutes. Let cool. Serve slices of tart with spoonfuls of apple compote.

Pimm's Trifle

PREPARATION TIME: 20 minutes, plus 15 minutes cooling time, 3½ hours setting time | COOKING TIME: 15 minutes |
SERVES: 4-6

16 ladyfingers
scant 1 cup heavy cream

PIMM'S GELATIN
6 gelatin sheets
scant 1 cup Pimm's No. 1
2½ cups lemon soda
1 small handful of micro
   mint, plus extra for
   decoration
11 ounces strawberries
   (about 2 cups)

CUSTARD
1 vanilla bean
3 egg yolks
¾ cup sugar
1 tablespoon cornstarch
1¼ cups full-fat milk
scant ½ cup heavy cream

There is nothing more English than Pimm's, apart from maybe the classic trifle. This delicious dessert combines the two and is great for a summertime treat.

To make the Pimm's gelatin, soak the gelatin sheets in a small bowl of cold water until softened, about 5 minutes. Mix the Pimm's and lemon soda together in a large bowl, then pour scant ½ cup of the mixture into a small saucepan. Bring just to a boil, then remove from the heat immediately. Squeeze the gelatin sheets to remove excess water, then stir into the heated Pimm's mixture until melted. Add the gelatin mix to the remaining cold Pimm's mix, then stir in the micro mint and strawberries.

Line a glass serving bowl with the ladyfingers, then pour in the Pimm's gelatin. Let cool. Cover with plastic wrap and refrigerate for 3 hours to set.

Using a sharp knife, split the vanilla bean in half and scrape the seeds into a heatproof bowl. Add the egg yolks, sugar and cornstarch and whisk together until combined. Pour the milk and cream into a nonstick saucepan and bring to a boil, then pour into the egg yolk mixture, stirring continuously so the eggs don't cook. Pour the custard mixture back into the saucepan and heat very gently, stirring continuously, until thickened. Let cool.

Pour the cooled custard over the set gelatin. Refrigerate for 30 minutes to set the custard.

Pour the cream into a bowl and whip until soft peaks form. Spoon evenly over the custard. Decorate with a sprinkling of micro mint and serve.

Maple Syrup Cheesecake

PREPARATION TIME: 20 minutes, plus minimum 6 hours setting time | COOKING TIME: 50 minutes | SERVES: 8

7 tablespoons unsalted butter, softened, plus extra for greasing
2¼ pounds cream cheese, softened
2 tablespoons cornstarch
½ cup sugar
1 cup maple syrup, plus extra for drizzling
1 vanilla bean
6 eggs
1¾ cups heavy cream
1 teaspoon lemon juice

FOR DECORATION
2 fuyu persimmons, quartered,
6 ground cherries/cape gooseberries, some in their papery casings
½ cup pecan halves

This is quick to cook and pretty foolproof. Unlike most cheesecakes, it doesn't have a base: it's just a large slab of creamy richness. The maple syrup adds caramel overtones and the pecans add crunch.

Preheat the oven to 350°F. Lightly grease a 10-inch springform cake pan. Wrap the base tightly with foil, then set the cake pan in a roasting pan.

Beat together the butter, cream cheese, cornstarch, sugar and maple syrup until well combined. Using a sharp knife, split the vanilla bean in half and scrape the seeds into the cream cheese mixture. Stir until the seeds are evenly incorporated. Add the eggs, one at a time, beating well after each addition, then pour in the cream and lemon juice and beat until all the ingredients are well combined.

Pour the mixture into the prepared cake pan. Pour enough boiling water into the roasting pan to come two-thirds of the way up the sides of the cake pan. Bake for 35 minutes, then turn the heat up to 400°F and continue baking until just set and golden around the edges, about 15 minutes longer.

Remove from the oven and let cool to room temperature, then cover with plastic wrap and refrigerate for at least 6 hours, or overnight, to set.

Remove the cheesecake from the pan and set on a serving plate. Decorate the top of the cheesecake with the persimmons, ground cherries and pecans and finish with a light drizzle of maple syrup before serving.

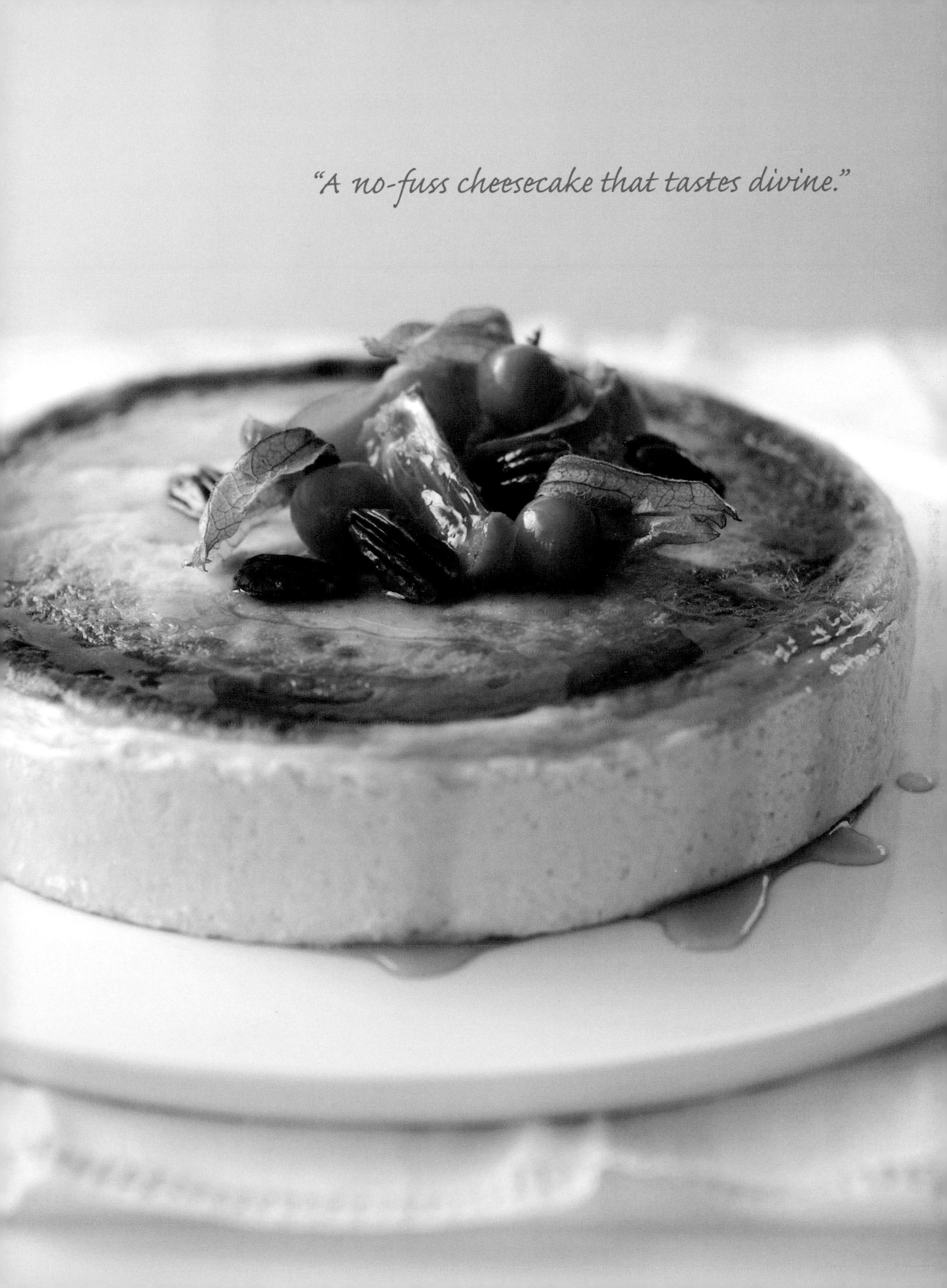
"A no-fuss cheesecake that tastes divine."

Mont Blanc Semifreddo

PREPARATION TIME: 20 minutes, plus 2 hours freezing time or overnight | COOKING TIME: 2¼ hours | SERVES: 8

4 eggs, separated
1¾ cups superfine sugar
1 teaspoon cornstarch
1 vanilla bean
2 cups heavy cream
2 tablespoons brandy
11 ounces sweetened
  chestnut purée

TO SERVE
about 5 ounces
  bittersweet chocolate,
  chopped (optional)

Preheat the oven to 275°F. Line two baking sheets with parchment paper. Using the base of a 10-inch springform cake pan as a guide, trace out two large circles on the paper. Also line the springform pan with parchment paper.

Put the egg whites in a large, clean bowl and beat until soft peaks form. Gradually add 1¼ cups of the sugar, a spoonful at a time, beating continuously, then continue beating until the sugar has completely dissolved and the meringue is thick and glossy. Beat in the cornstarch.

Pipe or spoon the meringue onto the baking sheets inside the traced circles, leaving a clear gap of about ½ inch between the meringue and the circle edge, to allow for expansion. Put the meringue disks in the oven and dry out until crisp, about 2 hours. Transfer to a wire rack and let cool completely.

Using a small sharp knife, split the vanilla bean in half and scrape the seeds into a bowl. Add the cream and whip to soft peaks. Set aside.

Put the egg yolks, remaining sugar and the brandy in a large heatproof bowl and set the bowl over a saucepan of gently boiling water, making sure the base of the bowl doesn't touch the water. Beat until the mixture is thick enough to leave a trail on its surface when the beaters are lifted out, 10–15 minutes. Fold the egg yolk mixture into the whipped cream, then fold in the chestnut purée. Don't mix the purée in completely, because it looks nicer a bit streaky.

Put one meringue disk in the springform pan and spoon in the chestnut cream mixture to cover. Top with the second meringue disk. Cover with foil and freeze for at least 2 hours or overnight. Remove from the freezer about 10 minutes before serving.

Put the chocolate (if using) in a heatproof bowl and set it over a saucepan of gently simmering water, making sure the base of the bowl doesn't touch the water. Heat, stirring occasionally, until the chocolate has melted. Drizzle the chocolate over the dessert just before serving.

Mango with Micro Basil Sorbet

PREPARATION TIME: 10 minutes, plus 30 minutes churning time and minimum 2 hours freezing time | COOKING TIME: 10 minutes | SERVES: 4

1¼ cups sugar
2 ounces micro basil leaves, plus 1 large handful
1 tablespoon lime juice
2 mangoes

This simple dish is very good as a dessert after a rich Asian dish. Micro basil has more of an aniseed flavor than normal basil, and it makes a palate-cleansing finale. You can, of course, use regular basil or Thai basil, if you prefer.

Put the sugar and 2 ounces micro basil into a saucepan with 1 cup water and bring to a boil. Turn the heat down and simmer for 10 minutes to infuse the liquid with the basil flavor. Remove from the heat and add the lime juice, then strain into a pitcher or bowl. Let cool. When the syrup is cold, add the remaining basil.

To make the sorbet using an ice-cream machine, pour the syrup into the bowl and churn according to the manufacturer's directions until it has a sorbet consistency. This will take about 30 minutes. Spoon the sorbet into a freezer container and freeze for at least 2 hours.

Alternatively, to still-freeze the sorbet, pour the syrup into a chilled freezer container, cover and freeze for 1½ hours. Remove from the freezer and stir the frozen edges into the rest of the mixture. Return to the freezer and repeat the stirring at hourly intervals two or three times. By now the sorbet should be completely frozen. (Note that the sorbet will not be quite as smooth as if made using an ice-cream machine.)

Using a sharp knife, carefully slice each mango down on either side of the pit. Peel the skin off the mango sides, then cut the flesh into slices. Peel the remaining parts of the mango and slice the flesh from the pit. Serve the mango topped with large scoops of sorbet.

Ginger Gelatins with Plum Purée & Micro Cilantro

PREPARATION TIME: 15 minutes, plus 5 hours setting time | COOKING TIME: 15 minutes | SERVES: 4

6 gelatin sheets
3¼ cups ginger ale
10 purple plums, pitted
  and cut into quarters
½ cup sugar
1 small handful of micro
  cilantro

I am asked to make a lot of healthy food for clients, and these desserts are perfect because they are fat-free. Cilantro may sound a bit odd here, but it does work, believe me.

Soak the gelatin sheets in a bowl of cold water until softened, about 5 minutes. Pour ⅔ cup of the ginger ale into a saucepan and bring to a boil. Remove the pan from the heat immediately. Squeeze the gelatin sheets to remove excess water, then stir into the hot ginger ale until completely melted. Mix with the remaining ginger ale. Pour into four 4-ounce molds. Let cool, then refrigerate for 4–5 hours to set.

Meanwhile, put the plums, sugar and scant ½ cup water in a saucepan over medium-high heat and bring to a boil. Reduce the heat to low and simmer until the plums are softened, about 10 minutes. Tip into a blender or food processor and blitz to a purée, then pass through a fine strainer into a bowl. Cover with plastic wrap and keep in the refrigerator until the gelatins are ready.

Unmold the gelatins onto four plates. Spoon the plum purée lightly over the top, then sprinkle with the micro cilantro and serve.

Poached Peaches with Honey Cream

PREPARATION TIME: 5 minutes | COOKING TIME: 25 minutes | SERVES: 4

1 cup sugar
4 white peaches
scant 1 cup heavy cream
1 tablespoon clear honey

TO SERVE
pistachio biscotti
   (optional)

This dish relies on the beauty of the fruit, so make it when fragrant white peaches are in season. You can also serve it with Greek yogurt for a healthy breakfast dish.

Pour 2 cups water into a saucepan, add the sugar and bring to a boil. Add the peaches, then reduce the heat to low and simmer until they are softened, about 10 minutes. Remove the peaches from the pan using a slotted spoon to a bowl. Simmer the poaching liquid until thick and syrupy, about 15 minutes. Pour the syrup over the peaches and set aside.

Pour the cream into a bowl and whip until soft peaks form. Add the honey and briefly whip again to combine.

Cut the peaches in half and remove the pits. Serve the peaches in syrup warm or cold, with the honey cream and with pistachio biscotti, if desired.

Blood Orange Tart

PREPARATION TIME: 20 minutes, plus making the pastry | COOKING TIME: 1 hour | SERVES: 8

1 recipe quantity Sweet
 Pastry dough (see
 page 202)
all-purpose flour, for
 dusting
1 cup sugar
7 eggs, plus 3 egg yolks,
 reserving a little egg
 white for brushing
grated zest and juice of
 2 lemons
scant 1 cup blood orange
 juice
scant 1 cup heavy cream

TO SERVE
crème fraîche

The classic lemon tart is one of life's best inventions, but I wanted to make something slightly different. Blood oranges are beautifully colored. Using them here results in a slightly softer citrus tart with a hint of blush.

Preheat the oven to 350°F. Roll out the pastry on a lightly floured surface until about ⅛ inch thick and large enough to line a 10-inch deep tart pan with a ¾-inch overhang. Carefully lift the pastry into the pan and press into the flutes; the pastry should rise slightly above the rim of the pan. Line the pastry shell with parchment paper and weight down with dried beans or rice.

Bake for 20 minutes, then remove the parchment paper and weights. Prick the bottom of the pastry shell with a fork and brush with beaten egg white. Return to the oven to bake until just starting to turn golden, about 5 minutes. Remove from the oven and set aside. Reduce the oven temperature to 275°F.

In a large bowl, beat the sugar, eggs and egg yolks together, then add the lemon zest and juice, orange juice and cream and beat until well combined.

Strain the citrus mixture into a pitcher or bowl, then pour into the pastry shell in an even layer. Bake until just set but still quite wobbly, about 30 minutes. Let cool before trimming the pastry to the height of the pan using a sharp knife. Serve each slice of tart with a dollop of crème fraîche.

Nectarine & Vanilla Clafoutis

PREPARATION TIME: 15 minutes | COOKING TIME: 30 minutes | SERVES: 4

butter, for greasing
2 nectarines,
    pitted and diced
3 eggs
scant ⅓ cup sugar, plus
    extra for sprinkling
1¼ cups milk
2 teaspoons vanilla
    extract
1 vanilla bean
6½ tablespoons
    self-rising flour
a pinch of kosher salt

Clafoutis is a classic French dessert that is surprisingly easy to make. It is usually made with cherries, but I love using ripe nectarines. It is the ultimate seasonal dessert, as it works with blackberries and raspberries too.

Preheat the oven to 350°F. Grease a 4-cup glass or ceramic baking dish with butter and spread the nectarines over the bottom.

Beat together the eggs and sugar in a large bowl until light and fluffy, then add the milk and vanilla and beat until well incorporated. Using a sharp knife, split the vanilla bean in half and scrape the seeds into the egg and sugar mixture. Beat again until the seeds are evenly incorporated.

Sift the flour and salt into the egg mixture, then very gently fold in the flour until well combined. Pour the batter over the nectarines. Bake until golden and risen, about 30 minutes.

Remove from the oven, sprinkle with sugar and serve immediately. The clafoutis will deflate a little as it cools.

Raspberry & Pistachio Meringue Pie

PREPARATION TIME: 20 minutes, plus making the pastry | COOKING TIME: 45 minutes | SERVES: 8

1 recipe quantity
  Sweet Pastry (see
  page 202)
all-purpose flour,
  for dusting
7 egg whites
1½ cups superfine sugar
1 tsp cornstarch
1 pound 2 ounces
  raspberries (heaped
  4 cups)
2 teaspoons chopped
  pistachio nuts

This is a quick version of the beloved lemon meringue pie. The raspberries piled up in the baked pastry case provide a perfect tart contrast to the sweet meringue and pistachios.

Preheat the oven to 350°F. Roll out the pastry on a lightly floured surface until about ⅛ inch thick and large enough to line a deep 8-inch loose-bottomed tart pan with a ¾-inch overhang. Carefully lift the pastry into the pan and press into the flutes; the pastry should rise slightly above the rim of the pan. Line the pastry shell with parchment paper and weight down with dried beans or rice.

Bake for 20 minutes, then remove the parchment paper and weights. Prick the bottom of the pastry shell with a fork. Whisk one of the egg whites with a fork and brush it over the bottom of the pastry shell. Return to the oven to bake until just starting to turn golden, about 5 minutes. Remove from the oven and reduce the oven temperature to 275°F. Let the pastry shell cool before trimming the pastry to the height of the pan using a sharp knife.

Meanwhile, put the remaining egg whites in a large clean bowl and beat until soft peaks form. Gradually add the sugar, a spoonful at a time, beating continuously, and continue beating until all the sugar has completely dissolved and the meringue is thick and glossy. Finally, beat in the cornstarch.

Spread the raspberries evenly in the pastry shell. Spoon the meringue over the raspberries, piling it up in the middle to form a high peak. Sprinkle with the pistachios. Bake until the meringue is lightly golden, about 20 minutes. Let cool before serving at room temperature.

Rosewater Pavlova

PREPARATION TIME: 25 minutes | COOKING TIME: 2 hours | SERVES: 4

6 extra-large egg whites
¾ cup superfine sugar
1 teaspoon cornstarch
1 teaspoon rosewater,
  plus an extra splash
a drizzle of grenadine
  syrup
1¼ cups heavy cream
1 teaspoon vanilla extract
7 ounces raspberries
  (about 1⅔ cups)

TO SERVE
1 small handful of rose
  petals (optional)

I adore dreamy, feminine desserts—dishes that wouldn't look out of place in a fairytale setting. This pavlova, with its pillows of rose-scented cream, raspberries and crisp pink meringue, is a real showstopper and it tastes magical, too.

Preheat the oven to 275°F and line two baking sheets with parchment paper. Put the egg whites in a large, clean mixing bowl and beat until soft peaks form. Beat in the sugar, a spoonful at a time, and continue beating until the meringue is thick and glossy. Add the cornstarch, rosewater and grenadine and mix well.

Spoon the meringue into a pastry bag and pipe an 8- to 10-inch disk on each lined baking sheet. Use the remainder to pipe small meringues around the meringue disks. Put into the oven and dry out the meringues for 1½ hours. Remove the mini meringues from the oven and let cool. Continue to dry the meringue disks for 30 minutes longer, then remove and let cool.

When the meringues are cold, whip the cream with a splash of rosewater and the vanilla until soft peaks form.

Put one of the meringue disks on a serving plate and cover with half the cream and raspberries. Place the second disk on top and cover with the remaining cream. Decorate with the remaining raspberries and the mini meringues. To finish, sprinkle the rose petals over before serving. (These are edible, but if you prefer not to eat them, just remove.)

Goat Cheese, Quince & Micro Celery Stacks

PREPARATION TIME: 15 minutes | COOKING TIME: 15 minutes | SERVES: 4

1 long, thin French
   baguette
1 teaspoon olive oil
14 ounces rindless goat
   cheese
1 tablespoon crème
   fraîche
7 ounces quince paste
4 ounces celery shoots
   (microgreen)
freshly ground black
   pepper

Sometimes I don't feel like making a sweet dessert but neither do I want to do without something a bit sweet. This is just right for those days: little layers of creamy goat cheese, slivers of quince and micro celery shoots for a sweet-savory delight.

Preheat the oven to 400°F. Cut the baguette on the diagonal into 12 very thin and long slices and spread the slices on a baking sheet. Drizzle the oil over. Bake until golden brown, 10–15 minutes. Remove from the oven and let cool.

Meanwhile, put the goat cheese and crème fraîche in a bowl and beat to make a piping consistency. Season with pepper. Cut the quince paste into slices of a similar size to the slices of baguette.

Spoon the goat cheese mixture into a pastry bag and pipe about 1 heaped teaspoon onto one slice of toasted baguette. Put a slice of quince paste on the cheese, then add another slice of toast, some more cheese and another slice of quince paste. Repeat once more, then finish with a little more cheese and sprinkle on one-quarter of the celery shoots. Make up the remaining three stacks in the same way, and serve.

Sfakian Cheese Pies

PREPARATION TIME: 45 minutes, plus 1 hour rising time | COOKING TIME: 40 minutes | MAKES: 8

1 egg
¼ cup olive oil
3²/₃ cups all-purpose flour,
   plus extra for dusting
1 teaspoon salt
1 pound 2 ounces mizithra
   or ricotta cheese (about
   2 cups)
oil, for frying

TO SERVE
strong Greek honey
thyme leaves
edible flowers (optional)

These pies are renowned in Crete, where they are mainly made in a remote area on the south of the island. While they do take some time to master, the thin bread with cheese in the middle, drizzled with honey, really takes some beating. I couldn't resist including them.

Whisk together the egg, oil and ½ cup water in a measure. Sift the flour and salt into a large bowl. Make a well in the flour, then pour in the liquid mixture. Knead the dry and wet ingredients together with your hands to make a smooth dough. Cover with a damp kitchen towel and let rest in a warm, draft-free place for 1 hour.

Divide the dough into eight pieces. Roll each piece into a ball on a lightly floured surface, then flatten slightly. Divide the mizithra or ricotta cheese into eight pieces and put one portion in the center of each dough ball. Wrap the dough around the cheese until it is completely enclosed.

Preheat the oven to 300°F and put a baking sheet in to warm. Take one dough ball and press down to flatten, then very gently and carefully roll it out into a thin pancake about the size of a side plate; turn the dough as you roll and make sure the cheese doesn't come out. Repeat with the remaining dough balls.

To cook the pies, heat a little oil in two frying pans over medium heat. Lay one pie in each pan and fry until lightly browned, about 5 minutes per side. Keep the pies warm on the hot baking sheet in the oven while you cook the remaining six pies.

Serve drizzled with honey and sprinkled with thyme leaves and edible flowers, if desired.

Wild Mushroom- & Truffle-Filled Camembert

PREPARATION TIME: 20 minutes, plus 1 hour chilling time and 30 minutes resting time | SERVES: 4

1 ounce dried wild
    mushrooms
4 ounces cream cheese
    (½ cup)
2 teaspoons truffle oil
9 ounces Camembert
    cheese
kosher salt and freshly
    ground black pepper

TO SERVE
crackers or French bread

I used to make a version of this in one of the Michelin-starred restaurants I worked in as a teenager. It's a wonderful combo of wild mushroom, truffle and cheese, and it oozes flavor.

Put the mushrooms in a heatproof bowl and pour in boiling water to cover. Let soak for 10 minutes, then drain. Chop the mushrooms finely and put back in the empty bowl.

Add the cream cheese and truffle oil to the mushrooms and season with salt and pepper. Mix until thoroughly combined.

Cut the Camembert in half horizontally, then sandwich the cream cheese mixture between the two halves. Cover with plastic wrap and refrigerate for 1 hour to chill.

Remove the stuffed Camembert from the refrigerator at least 30 minutes before serving, to bring it to room temperature. Serve with crackers or slices of crusty French bread.

"If you bought this in a deli, it would cost a fortune!"

Baking

Za'atar Flatbreads

PREPARATION TIME: 40 minutes, plus 2½ hours rising time | COOKING TIME: 1 hour 5 minutes | MAKES: 8

1 teaspoon active dry yeast
3 cups wholewheat flour
1¼ cups white bread flour, plus extra for dusting
1 teaspoon kosher salt
2 tablespoons cornstarch

ZA'ATAR MIX
2 tablespoons toasted sesame seeds
2 teaspoons dried thyme
2 teaspoons chopped fresh thyme
2 teaspoons sumac
1 teaspoon sea salt crystals

Dissolve the yeast in 1 cup lukewarm water in a small pitcher. Sift the wholewheat and white flours together into a large bowl (tip in the bran left in the sifter) and add the salt.

Make a well in the center of the flours and pour in the yeast mixture. Knead the dry and wet ingredients together with your hands to make a soft dough—you may need to add another 1–2 tablespoons water if it is too dry. Turn the dough onto a lightly floured surface and knead until smooth and elastic, 5–10 minutes longer. Put the dough in a bowl lightly dusted with flour, cover with a damp, clean kitchen towel and let rise in a warm, draft-free place until the dough has doubled in size, 1½–2 hours.

Meanwhile, combine all the ingredients for the za'atar mix in a bowl.

Punch down the dough, then turn it out onto a lightly floured surface and mold into a long sausage shape. Pinch off eight equal-sized pieces of dough. Roll each into a ball, then roll the dough balls in the cornstarch to coat all over. Put the balls on a baking sheet lightly dusted with flour, cover with a damp, clean kitchen towel and let rise in the warm, draft-free place for 30 minutes.

On a clean surface, press down a dough ball with the palm of your hand a few times, rotating the dough a little after each press. Pick up the flattened piece of dough and shift it from one hand to the other, using a swift motion, to stretch it. Put the dough back on the surface and, using a rolling pin, roll it out as thinly as possible. Repeat for the remaining dough balls.

Heat a large nonstick frying pan over medium heat. Put a flatbread in the pan and cook until browned, about 5 minutes. Flip the bread over, spread 1 teaspoon of the za'atar mix over the browned side and fry until cooked through, about 3 more minutes. Repeat for the remaining flatbreads, piling them up under a damp kitchen towel as they are cooked to keep warm before serving.

Chili & Cilantro Cornbread

PREPARATION TIME: 15 minutes | COOKING TIME: 20 minutes | SERVES: 4

9 tablespoons (1 stick +
  1 tablespoon) butter,
  melted, plus extra for
  greasing
½ cup + 2 tablespoons
  sugar
2 eggs
scant 1¼ cups buttermilk
½ teaspoon baking soda
1⅔ cups self-rising flour
2 cups fine cornmeal
½ teaspoon salt
1 tablespoon minced
  pickled jalapeño
1 small handful of micro
  cilantro
1 cup shredded Cheddar
  cheese

Cornbread was one of the first breads I learned to make as a child, and its buttery goodness has been a favorite ever since. There are lots of different recipes—this one is simple and very quick, and the cornbread should be eaten warm. It can be easily varied: try adding crisp bacon pieces and other cheeses.

Preheat the oven to 350°F and grease a 13- by 8-inch baking pan with plenty of butter. Beat the butter and sugar together in a large bowl, then add the eggs, one at a time, mixing well after each addition.

Pour the buttermilk into another bowl, add the baking soda and stir well, then stir into the butter mixture. Sift in the flour and add the cornmeal and salt. Stir until well combined. Finally, add the jalapeño, micro cilantro and Cheddar.

Pour the batter into the prepared pan and bake until risen and golden brown, about 20 minutes. Remove the cornbread from the oven and let cool slightly in the pan, then cut into wedges or squares and serve warm.

Oaty Soda Bread

PREPARATION TIME: 15 minutes | COOKING TIME: 30 minutes | MAKES: 1 loaf

2/3 cup old-fashioned
   rolled oats
2 cups wholewheat flour
1 1/3 cups all-purpose flour,
   plus extra for dusting
1 teaspoon baking soda
1 teaspoon sugar
1 teaspoon salt
2 tablespoons butter,
   melted
1 3/4 cups buttermilk
   (or mix together
   1 1/4 cups milk with
   1/2 cup plain yogurt)

For me, there really is nothing better than warm soda bread with butter and jam for breakfast. It is a very quick bread to make. I have added oats to this recipe for some extra texture and fiber, which will also keep you fuller for longer.

Preheat the oven to 350°F. Put the oats into a food processor and pulse until finely chopped to a meal.

Combine the oatmeal, wholewheat and all-purpose flours, baking soda, sugar and salt in a large bowl and mix until well combined.

Mix together the butter and buttermilk in a measure. Make a well in the dry ingredients and gradually pour in the buttermilk, bringing the dry ingredients into the buttermilk with your hands. Continue mixing until just combined; don't overwork the dough.

Turn the oaty dough onto a lightly floured surface and mold into a round loaf shape. Cut a deep cross in the center and dust the top with flour, then set the loaf on a baking sheet. Bake until golden brown, about 30 minutes. Remove from the oven and let cool a little on a wire rack. Serve warm.

Cinnamon, Date & Cardamom Rolls

PREPARATION TIME: 30 minutes, plus 2½ hours rising time | COOKING TIME: 25 minutes | MAKES: 8

1¼ cups milk
1 package active dry yeast
4 eggs
½ cup sugar
7 tablespoons unsalted
  butter, melted
5½ cups all-purpose
  flour, plus extra for
  dusting

FILLING
2 tablespoons ground
  cinnamon
1 teaspoon ground
  cardamom
1 heaped cup chopped
  dates
½ cup packed raw sugar,
  such as turbinado
1 teaspoon vanilla extract
14 tablespoons (1 stick +
  6 tablespoons) butter

CINNAMON GLAZE
2 teaspoons ground
  cinnamon
2 cups sugar

The smell of cinnamon rolls seems to have a sort of hypnotic effect on people. Instead of the usual raisins, I have used toffee-like dates and added a little cardamom, then finished the rolls with a sticky glaze.

Warm the milk in a saucepan over medium heat. Remove from the heat and stir in the yeast. Set aside to dissolve.

Put the eggs, sugar and melted butter in a large measure and mix together, then whisk in the warmed milk-yeast mixture. Sift the flour into a large bowl, make a well in the center and pour in the egg mixture. Bring the dry and wet ingredients together to make a rough, sticky dough. Turn the dough onto a lightly floured work surface and knead until the dough is smooth and elastic, about 5 minutes.

Put the dough in a clean bowl, cover with a damp kitchen towel and let rise in a warm, draft-free place until the dough has doubled in size, 1½–2 hours. Meanwhile, mix together all the filling ingredients, except the butter, in a bowl. Put the butter in a saucepan and melt, then tip it into the bowl and stir until well combined. Set aside.

Punch down the dough, then turn it onto a lightly floured surface and knead slightly. Roll out until about ½ inch thick. Spread the filling over in an even layer and roll up the dough. Cut across into 2-inch pieces and arrange them, cut-side up, in a 10-inch round cake pan. Cover with a damp kitchen towel and let rise in the warm, draft-free place for 30 minutes.

Preheat the oven to 400°F. Bake the rolls until golden brown and risen, about 20 minutes. Meanwhile, put the cinnamon and sugar for the glaze in a saucepan with scant ½ cup water. Bring to a boil, then reduce the heat to low and simmer until slightly thickened, about 10 minutes. When the rolls are cooked, remove from the oven and drizzle the syrup over. Let cool in the pan before serving.

Orange-Blossom Éclairs

PREPARATION TIME: 25 minutes, plus chilling time | COOKING TIME: 35 minutes | MAKES: 14

oil, for greasing
2 tablespoons unsalted
    butter
½ cup all-purpose flour,
    plus extra for dusting
2 eggs, beaten
scant 1 cup heavy cream
scant ½ cup
    confectioners' sugar
½ tablespoon orange-
    flower water

ICING
1²/₃ cups confectioners'
    sugar

TO DECORATE
edible gold leaf,
    (optional)

These were inspired by a Middle-Eastern dessert called *atayef bi ashta*, which is often served during Ramadan, after the sun has gone down. I adore the orange-blossom-flavored custard and have added some gold leaf for a luxurious Arabian touch.

Preheat the oven to 400°F, and lightly oil and flour a baking sheet.

Pour ²/₃ cup water into a saucepan, add the butter and bring to a boil. Reduce the heat to medium, then, stirring vigorously and continuously, add the flour in one quick burst. Continue stirring until a soft paste forms and the oil from the butter starts to come to the surface. Remove the saucepan from the heat. Gradually beat in the eggs until the choux paste is smooth and glossy, and thick enough to drop off the spoon with a gentle shake. Let cool.

Spoon the choux paste into a large pastry bag fitted with a ¾-inch plain tip and pipe 3¼-inch lengths on the prepared baking sheet, leaving space between them because the éclairs will double in size during baking. Bake until golden brown and crisp, about 30 minutes.

Remove the éclairs from the oven, pierce the bases with a skewer to release the steam and let cool completely on a wire rack.

Whip the cream and confectioners' sugar together in a bowl until stiff peaks form. Mix in the orange-flower water, then spoon the cream into a pastry bag fitted with a plain tip. Pierce the base of each éclair with the tip and pipe in the cream. Refrigerate.

To make the icing, mix together the sugar and 1 tablespoon water in a bowl. Dip the top of the éclairs in the icing, or spread the icing using a thin metal spatula. Let set, then sprinkle with edible gold leaf, if desired, before serving.

Iced Fancies

PREPARATION TIME: 1 hour | COOKING TIME: 50 minutes | MAKES: 16

2 tablespoons unsalted
    butter, melted and
    cooled, plus extra
    for greasing
4 eggs
½ cup granulated sugar
½ teaspoon almond
    extract
6½ tablespoons
    cornstarch
⅓ cup self-rising flour
¼ cup raspberry jam,
    warmed
6 ounces marzipan
confectioners' sugar,
    for dusting

ICING
4 cups fondant
    sugar (very fine
    confectioners'/
    powdered sugar for
    fondant icing)
pink, green, blue and
    yellow food coloring

Preheat the oven to 350°F, and grease and line an 8-inch square cake pan with parchment paper. Break the eggs into a large heatproof bowl, add the granulated sugar and set the bowl over a saucepan of simmering water, making sure the base of the bowl doesn't touch the water. Using a portable electric mixer, beat until the mixture doubles in volume, 5–8 minutes.

Remove the bowl from the heat, add the melted butter and almond extract and stir until well combined. Then, using a metal spoon, very gently fold in the cornstarch and flour. Pour the batter into the prepared cake pan.

Bake until lightly golden and a skewer inserted into the center comes out clean, 30–40 minutes. Remove the cake from the oven and unmold onto a wire rack to cool completely. When cold, slice in half horizontally and sandwich the two halves together with the jam, reserving 1 tablespoon. Trim off the edges and cut into sixteen 2-inch squares.

Roll out the marzipan on a surface lightly dusted with confectioners' sugar until about ⅛ inch thick. Spread the reserved jam evenly over the top. Cut the marzipan into 16 squares to fit the tops of the individual cakes. Put one square of marzipan, jam-side down, on each cake.

To make the icing, mix the fondant sugar with enough hot water to make a smooth and thick yet pourable consistency. Divide the icing equally among four bowls. Mix a few drops of food coloring into each bowl to make up soft pastel pink, green, blue and yellow icings. Cover the bowls with plastic wrap to prevent a skin from forming on the icings.

Put the prepared cakes, marzipan-side up, on a wire rack set over a baking sheet. Pour one of the colored icings over four of the cakes, using a thin metal spatula to smooth it down the sides. Repeat with the remaining icings until all the cakes are coated. Let set before serving.

"These gorgeous pastel-colored, bite-size cakes are just perfect for afternoon tea."

Coconut & Lime Cake

PREPARATION TIME: 25 minutes, plus making the coconut shavings | COOKING TIME: 35 minutes | SERVES: 8

1 cup (2 sticks) unsalted butter, softened, plus extra for greasing
1 cup + 2 tablespoons sugar
4 eggs
grated zest of 1 lime
6 ounces creamed coconut block, grated
3 tablespoons coconut milk
1½ cups self-rising flour

FROSTING
1 cup sugar
2 egg whites
1 tablespoon Malibu rum liqueur

TO DECORATE
1 ounce toasted fresh coconut shavings, (see page 154)

Coconut and lime go so well together. The creamed coconut makes a very moist cake and the frosting is light and fluffy.

Preheat the oven to 350°F, and grease and line a 9-inch round cake pan with parchment paper.

Beat together the butter and sugar in a bowl until light and fluffy. Lightly beat the eggs in another bowl, then gradually add to the creamed butter mixture, beating well after each addition to prevent the mixture from curdling. Beat in the lime zest (reserving a few strands for decorating) and the creamed coconut, followed by the coconut milk, then gently fold in the flour until everything is well combined.

Pour the batter into the prepared cake pan and bake until golden and a skewer inserted into the center comes out clean, about 30 minutes. Remove from the oven and unmold onto a wire rack to cool completely.

To make the frosting, put the sugar in a saucepan with ¼ cup water and stir to dissolve over medium heat, then bring to a boil. Boil for 4 minutes to form a syrup. Meanwhile, beat the egg whites in a large, clean bowl until firm. Pouring in a slow, steady stream, add the sugar syrup to the egg whites, beating until the frosting is thick and glossy. Finally, beat in the Malibu.

Slice the cake in half horizontally and place the bottom half on a serving plate. Add a thick layer of the warm frosting, then set the other cake layer on top. Cover the sides and top of the cake with the remaining frosting. Decorate with the coconut shavings and the reserved lime zest. Let the frosting cool and set before serving.

189

Rich Flourless Chocolate Cake

PREPARATION TIME: 20 minutes, plus 45 minutes cooling | COOKING TIME: 35 minutes | SERVES: 8

5 ounces semisweet
   chocolate with 50%
   cacao, chopped
1 cup (2 sticks) unsalted
   butter, softened, plus
   extra for greasing
1 teaspoon sea salt
   crystals
4 eggs, separated
1 cup sugar
1 teaspoon vanilla extract

TO SERVE
crème fraîche

I try to avoid eating much wheat, and I have had many clients who do the same, so here is a no-flour cake, which is super-rich and decadent. Serve each slice with a dollop of crème fraîche.

Preheat the oven to 325°F, and grease and line a 6-inch round cake pan with parchment paper. Put the chocolate and butter in a heatproof bowl and set it over a saucepan of gently simmering water, making sure the base of the bowl doesn't touch the water. Heat, stirring occasionally, until the chocolate and butter have melted, then stir in the salt. Set aside.

Beat the egg yolks with half of the sugar until the mixture is pale and thick. Put the egg whites in another clean, large bowl and beat until soft peaks form, then add the remaining sugar, a spoonful at a time, beating continuously. Continue beating until all the sugar has completely dissolved and the mixture is thick and glossy.

Stir the melted chocolate and butter into the egg yolk mixture and add the vanilla, then gently fold in the egg whites until well combined.

Pour the batter into the prepared cake pan and bake until firm to the touch and a skewer inserted into the center of the cake comes out clean, about 30 minutes. Unmold the cake onto a wire rack to cool completely.

Serve the cake at room temperature, or chill first for a more dense texture.

LOVE GOOD FOOD

Lemon-Meringue Cupcakes

PREPARATION TIME: 25 minutes | COOKING TIME: 20 minutes | MAKES: 10

7½ tablespoons unsalted butter, softened
½ cup + 1 tablespoon granulated sugar
2 eggs
1 teaspoon vanilla extract
⅔ cup self-rising flour
½ teaspoon baking powder
2 tablespoons milk
4 ounces lemon curd (scant ½ cup)

MERINGUE
2 egg whites
heaped ½ cup superfine sugar

Cupcakes are very popular, and I have seen some mad creations. Here, the combination of soft sponge cake with lemon curd and meringue topping is simply lovely.

Preheat the oven to 350°F, and line a 12-cup muffin pan with paper liners.

Beat the butter with the sugar until light and fluffy. Lightly beat the eggs together in another bowl, then gradually add to the creamed butter mixture, beating well between each addition to prevent the mixture from curdling. Beat in the vanilla.

Sift the flour and baking powder together into the wet ingredients and gently fold in until all the flour has been incorporated. Finally, fold in the milk. Spoon the mixture into the muffin cases, filling each one about two-thirds full. Bake until risen and golden brown, about 10 minutes.

Remove the cupcakes from the oven, leaving the oven on. Let the cupcakes cool slightly, then scoop out (and discard) a teaspoon of cake from the middle of each one. Fill each hole with 1–2 heaped teaspoons lemon curd.

To make the meringue, put the egg whites in a dry, clean bowl and beat until soft peaks form. Gradually add the sugar, a spoonful at a time, beating continuously, and continue beating until all the sugar has completely dissolved and the meringue is thick and glossy.

Spoon the meringue into a pastry bag fitted with a plain tip. Neatly pipe a little mound of meringue over the lemon curd on top of each cupcake, leaving a gap around the edges. Put the cupcakes back into the oven and bake until the meringue tops are lightly golden, about 10 minutes. Remove from the oven and let cool before serving.

Mayan Chocolate Cupcakes

PREPARATION TIME: 25 minutes | COOKING TIME: 20 minutes | MAKES: 12

7½ tablespoons unsalted butter, softened

½ cup + 1 tablespoon packed light brown sugar

4 ounces bittersweet chocolate with 70% cacao, chopped

2 eggs

1 teaspoon vanilla extract

1 hot red chili, seeded and minced

⅔ cup self-rising flour

½ teaspoon baking powder

1 teaspoon ground cinnamon

1 teaspoon apple-pie spice

1 teaspoon grated orange zest

2 tablespoons milk

FROSTING

1¼ cups heavy cream

7 ounces bittersweet chocolate with 70% cacao, finely chopped

1 tablespoon honey

FOR DECORATION

12 slivers of seeded hot red chili

12 pink peppercorns

ground cinnamon, for sprinkling

edible gold dust, for sprinkling (optional)

To make the frosting, pour the cream into a saucepan set over medium heat and bring to a gentle boil, then immediately remove from the heat. Stir the chocolate into the cream, mixing until melted, then stir in the honey. Let cool until the frosting has a thick, piping consistency, 45 minutes to 1 hour.

While the frosting is cooling, make the cupcakes. Preheat the oven to 350°F, and line a 12-cup muffin pan with paper liners. Beat together the butter and sugar until light and fluffy.

Put the chocolate in a small heatproof bowl and set it over a saucepan of gently simmering water, making sure the base of the bowl doesn't touch the water. Heat, stirring occasionally, until the chocolate has melted. (Alternatively, melt the chocolate in a glass bowl in the microwave in 1-minute spurts, checking frequently.) Remove from the heat.

Lightly beat the eggs together in another bowl, then gradually add to the creamed butter mixture, beating well after each addition to prevent the mixture from curdling. Beat in the vanilla, melted chocolate and chili.

Sift the flour, baking powder, cinnamon and apple-pie spice into the wet ingredients and add the orange zest. Gently fold together until all the dry ingredients have been incorporated. Finally, fold in the milk.

Spoon the mixture into the muffin cases, filling each one about two-thirds full. Bake until risen and springy to the touch, about 10 minutes. Transfer the cupcakes, in their paper cases, to a wire rack to cool completely.

Pipe the cooled frosting in swirls over the tops of the cupcakes, using a pastry bag fitted with a star tip. Alternatively, spread the frosting over the tops using a thin metal spatula. Decorate each cupcake with a sliver of chili and a peppercorn, and sprinkle with cinnamon and edible gold dust before serving, if using.

"The Mayans worshipped chocolate, and magically combined it with chili and spices."

Caramel Cookie Sandwiches

PREPARATION TIME: 25 minutes, plus 30 minutes chilling time | COOKING TIME: 20 minutes | MAKES: 20

1 cup (2 sticks) unsalted butter, softened
½ cup + 1½ tablespoons packed light brown sugar
2 egg yolks
2 cups all-purpose flour, sifted, plus extra for dusting
6 ounces dulce de leche
sea-salt flakes (optional)
14 ounces milk chocolate, chopped

Buttery sablé cookies, sweet caramel and a layer of chocolate... what can I say? These are the perfect cookies.

Preheat the oven to 325°F, and line two baking sheets with parchment paper. Beat the butter with the sugar until light and fluffy, then add the egg yolks, one at a time, mixing well after each addition.

Add the flour to the butter mixture and mix until it just forms a paste. Do not overmix or the dough will be tough when cooked. Shape the dough into a ball, wrap in plastic wrap and refrigerate for 30 minutes to firm up.

Roll out the chilled dough on a lightly floured surface until about ¼ inch thick. (The dough is very short, so it may be easier to do this in batches.) Using a 2½-inch round cookie cutter, cut out 40 circles and put them on the lined baking sheets. Bake until lightly golden, 10–15 minutes. Remove from the oven and transfer the cookies to a wire rack to cool.

When the cookies are cold, sandwich pairs together with a spoonful of dulce de leche, leaving them on the wire rack. If desired, before sandwiching the cookies together, sprinkle a little salt over the dulce de leche.

Put the chocolate in a heatproof bowl and set it over a saucepan of gently simmering water, making sure the base of the bowl doesn't touch the water. Heat, stirring occasionally, until the chocolate has melted. (Alternatively, melt the chocolate in a glass bowl in the microwave in 1-minute spurts, checking progress frequently.)

Carefully spoon the melted chocolate over the tops of the cookies. Let cool, then transfer to another rack or plate and refrigerate to set, before serving.

Honey Madeleines with Earl-Grey Cream

PREPARATION TIME: 20 minutes, plus overnight chilling time | COOKING TIME: 10 minutes | MAKES: 24

4 eggs
heaped ¾ cup
  confectioners' sugar
2 tablespoons honey
1 teaspoon grated
  orange zest
1 teaspoon vanilla extract
1⅓ cups all-purpose
  flour, sifted
½ teaspoon baking
  powder
1 cup + 2 tablespoons (2
  sticks + 2 tablespoons)
  unsalted butter, melted,
  plus extra for greasing

EARL-GREY CREAM
2 teaspoons Earl Grey tea
  leaves
scant 1 cup heavy cream
scant ¼ cup
  confectioners' sugar

Madeleines were made famous by Proust and his memories invoked by them. You can tell why—they fill the house with a wonderful buttery fragrance. The scented Earl-Grey cream is a perfect partner. In Greece, I serve them with candied bergamot peel in syrup, too.

Put the eggs and sugar in a bowl and beat until light and fluffy and doubled in volume. Add the honey, orange zest and vanilla, then fold in the flour and baking powder until well combined. Stir in the melted butter. Transfer the batter to a clean bowl, cover with plastic wrap and refrigerate overnight.

Preheat the oven to 350°F, and brush a 24-cup madeleine mold (or two 12-cup molds) with butter. Spoon the batter into the molds to fill them about three-quarters full. Bake until golden, about 10 minutes. Remove from the oven and unmold the madeleines onto a wire rack to cool a little.

To make the Earl-Grey cream, infuse the tea leaves in 3 tablespoons boiling water until the water has cooled. Whip the cream with the sugar in a bowl until stiff peaks will form. Strain the tea infusion into the cream and whip until combined. Serve with the warm madeleines.

Basics

The following recipes are used as part of some of the main recipes. They are also a selection of deliciously handy recipes that will work as part of any number of different meals you may make at home, from your own special homemade pizza and pasta dishes to simply broiled meats and vegetables.

BBQ Sauce

PREPARATION TIME: 5 minutes | COOKING TIME: 50 minutes | MAKES: 2 cups

1 teaspoon vegetable oil
2 large shallots, finely chopped
2 cups ketchup
$2/3$ cup cider vinegar
2 tablespoons dark molasses
1 cup packed brown sugar
1 teaspoon cayenne
2 teaspoons celery salt
2 teaspoons prepared English mustard

Heat the oil in a saucepan over medium heat. Add the shallots and cook gently, covered, until softened and translucent, about 8 minutes.

Add the rest of the ingredients and mix well. Bring to a boil, then reduce the heat to low and simmer very gently, uncovered, stirring occasionally, until thick and glossy, 30–40 minutes. Because of the high sugar content the mixture will burn easily, so keep the heat low. Let cool.

The sauce can be kept in a tightly covered container in the refrigerator for 2–3 weeks.

Dipping Sauce

PREPARATION TIME: 5 minutes

1 hot red chili, finely chopped
1-inch piece of fresh gingerroot, peeled and finely chopped
1 tablespoon soy sauce
1 teaspoon fish sauce
1 teaspoon mirin
2 tablespoons rice vinegar

Put all the ingredients in a small bowl and whisk until thoroughly combined. Use immediately, or cover and keep in a cool place until needed.

Mayonnaise

PREPARATION TIME: 10 minutes | MAKES: 1¼ cups

2 egg yolks
1 tablespoon white wine
   vinegar
1 teaspoon Dijon mustard
scant 1 cup vegetable oil
5 teaspoons olive oil
a squeeze of lemon juice,
   to taste
a pinch of cayenne
kosher salt
2 garlic cloves, finely
   chopped (optional)

Put the egg yolks, vinegar and mustard in a food processor or blender and blitz until pale. With the motor running, pour in the oils—first the vegetable oil and then the olive oil—very slowly. If you add the oil too quickly, the mayonnaise could split.

When all the oil has been incorporated, add the lemon juice and cayenne, then season with salt. The mayonnaise can be kept, in a covered container, in the refrigerator for up to 4 days.

For garlic mayonnaise, add the garlic cloves with the mustard.

Yogurt Sauce

PREPARATION TIME: 5 minutes | MAKES: 1¼ cups

scant 1 cup Greek yogurt
1 garlic clove, finely
   chopped
1 teaspoon honey
1 tablespoon tahini

Put all the ingredients into a bowl and whisk together until thoroughly combined.

The sauce is best used on the day it is made.

Pineapple & Chili Sambal

PREPARATION TIME: 10 minutes | SERVES: 4

1 shallot, finely sliced
1 hot red chili, seeded and
   finely sliced
2 cups fresh pineapple,
   cut into small pieces

Put all the ingredients in a large bowl and toss until well combined.

The sambal is best used on the day it is made.

Curry Paste

PREPARATION TIME: 5 minutes

2-inch piece of fresh
   gingerroot, peeled and
   roughly chopped
2 large shallots, peeled
4 garlic cloves, peeled
1 hot red chili, seeded
1-inch piece of galangal,
   peeled and sliced
½ teaspoon each ground
   turmeric, ground cumin,
   ground coriander and
   hot chili powder
2 tablespoons coconut
   milk

Put all the ingredients in a blender or food processor and blitz until very smooth.

The paste is best used on the day it is made but can be kept in a tightly covered container for 2–3 days.

Quick Tomato Chutney

PREPARATION TIME: 5 minutes | COOKING TIME: 40 minutes | MAKES: generous 2 cups

2 large shallots, chopped
28 ounces canned
   crushed tomatoes
1 teaspoon yellow
   mustard seeds
½ teaspoon smoked
   paprika
1 cup packed brown sugar
⅔ cup white wine vinegar
½ teaspoon kosher salt

Put all the ingredients in a large saucepan and bring to a boil. Reduce the heat to low and simmer, stirring occasionally, until reduced, thick and glossy, about 40 minutes. Remove from the heat and let cool.

The chutney can be kept in a tightly covered container in the refrigerator for 2–3 weeks.

Deluxe Burger Buns

PREPARATION TIME: 30 minutes, plus 4 hours rising time | COOKING TIME: 40 minutes | MAKES: 8

3 tablespoons milk,
   warmed
1 teaspoon sugar
2 teaspoons active
   dry yeast
scant 4 cups white bread
   flour, plus extra for
   dusting
1 teaspoon salt
2 tablespoons butter
1 egg, plus 1 egg yolk for
   brushing
sesame seeds, poppy
   seeds or black onion
   seeds, for sprinkling

Mix together the milk, 1 cup warm water, the sugar and yeast in a small bowl and let prove for 5 minutes. Sift the flour and salt into a large bowl. Rub in the butter with your fingertips until the mixture resembles fine bread crumbs.

Whisk the whole egg into the yeast mixture. Make a well in the flour mixture and pour in the yeast mixture. Mix the dry and wet ingredients together, using your hands, to make a rough, sticky dough. Turn the dough onto a lightly floured work surface and knead until the dough is smooth and elastic, about 10 minutes.

Put the dough in a clean, oiled bowl, and lightly oil the top of the dough. Cover with a damp kitchen towel and leave in a warm, draft-free place until the dough has doubled in size, 1½–2 hours.

Line a baking sheet with parchment paper, or oil and lightly dust with flour. Punch down the dough, then turn it onto a lightly floured work surface and knead again for 5 minutes. Divide the dough into eight pieces and knead each a little more, then mold into bun shapes. Put the buns at least 2 inches apart on the baking sheet, cover with a kitchen towel and let rise in the warm, draft-free place for 1½–2 hours. The buns need to be a lot bigger before they are cooked, so don't be tempted to rush this stage otherwise they will be tough.

Preheat the oven to 350°F, and put a roasting pan filled with water on the bottom (this is to create moisture and keep the crust chewy). Brush the buns with the beaten egg yolk and sprinkle with sesame seeds, poppy seeds or black onion seeds. Bake until golden brown, 30–40 minutes. Transfer to a wire rack to cool.

Note that for my Lobster Rolls with Pea Shoots (see page 66), you need to form the dough into hotdog buns rather than round buns.

Flatbreads

PREPARATION TIME: 15 minutes, plus 15 minutes resting time | COOKING TIME: 15 minutes | MAKES: 4

scant 3½ cups 00 pasta
  flour, plus extra for
  dusting
1 egg, beaten
1 cup plain yogurt
3½ tablespoons olive oil,
  plus extra for oiling
kosher salt

Put all the ingredients in a stand mixer fitted with a dough hook and mix to a smooth dough. Turn the dough into a lightly oiled bowl, cover with plastic wrap and refrigerate for at least 15 minutes. If more convenient, you can make the dough the day before and leave in the refrigerator overnight.

Roll and bake the flatbreads according to the recipes on pages 43 and 179. Alternatively, for plain flatbreads, preheat the oven to 350°F. Roll out the dough on a lightly floured surface, then divide the dough according to the size of flatbread required and flatten into thin disks. Put the disks on a baking sheet and bake until golden brown, 10–15 minutes.

Sweet Pastry Dough

PREPARATION TIME: 10 minutes, plus 30 minutes chilling time | MAKES: about 13 ounces

9 tablespoons (1 stick +
  1 tablespoon) unsalted
  butter, softened
¼ cup sugar
1 vanilla bean
1 extra-large egg
1¾ cups pastry flour, plus
  extra for dusting

Put the butter and sugar in a mixing bowl. Using a sharp knife, split the vanilla bean in half and scrape the seeds into the bowl. Beat the ingredients together until smooth.

Add the egg and beat briefly until incorporated into the butter mixture, then add the flour and beat until just combined. Don't overbeat the mixture or the pastry will be tough.

Turn the dough onto a lightly floured surface and quickly shape into a ball. Wrap in plastic wrap and refrigerate for at least 30 minutes before using.

Pasta Dough

PREPARATION TIME: 40 minutes, plus 30 minutes resting time | SERVES: 4

5¼ cups 00 pasta flour,
  plus extra for dusting
1 teaspoon kosher salt
5 eggs, plus 1 egg yolk for
  brushing
1 tablespoon olive oil

Sift the flour and salt into a pile on a clean work surface, then make a well in the center of the flour. Whisk the eggs and olive oil together in a small bowl, then pour the liquid into the well. Using your hands, gradually bring the flour into the liquid to start to form a rough dough, then knead the dough until it is smooth. Shape into a ball, wrap in plastic wrap and let rest in the refrigerator for 30 minutes.

Now you need to gradually roll the dough until it is about ⅛ inch thick. If you have a pasta machine, it is easy, but if you are going to use a rolling pin, it will take some time and effort.

If using a pasta machine, cut the dough in half and set one half aside under a damp kitchen towel. Roll out the first half on a lightly floured surface until about ½ inch thick. Set up the pasta machine according to the manufacturer's handbook, ensuring it is securely attached to a clean work surface with lots of space around it. Set the machine to its widest setting, and dust the rollers and the work surface with flour. Feed the pasta dough into the machine, rolling it through the machine once, then fold it in half and roll it again. Turn the machine down a setting. Fold the dough in half and roll it twice on this setting, folding it in half each time. At this point you will probably have to cut the sheet in half because of its length; cover the remainder of the sheet with a damp kitchen towel to keep it from drying out while you carry on rolling. Turn the machine down another setting and roll the dough twice more. Continue until you have rolled the dough through the finest setting twice. Repeat the rolling process with the remaining dough.

If making ravioli, use the whole sheets of pasta. If making fettucine, tagliatelle or other pasta shapes, either pass the dough through the pasta machine using the correct cutting attachment, or fold the sheets in half a few times and cut with a knife, using a ruler to keep the strips even.

Pizza Dough

PREPARATION TIME: 30 minutes, plus minimum 2 hours rising time | MAKES: 4 small pizzas or 1 large pizza

1 package active dry yeast
4 cups all-purpose flour,
    plus extra for dusting
1 teaspoon sugar
1 tablespoon kosher salt
3 tablespoons olive oil
semolina or cornmeal,
    for dusting

Mix the yeast with 1½ cups warm water in a small bowl. Put the flour, sugar and salt in a large bowl and mix well. Make a well in the center of the flour mixture and pour in the yeast mixture and the olive oil. Mix the dry and wet ingredients together, using your hands, to make a rough dough. Turn the dough onto a lightly floured work surface and knead until the dough is smooth and elastic, about 10 minutes. Put the dough in a clean, oiled bowl, and lightly oil the top of the dough. Cover with a damp kitchen towel and let rise in a warm, draft-free place until doubled in size, about 2 hours.

Punch down the dough and knead for 5 minutes, but this time on a surface lightly dusted with semolina. Divide the dough into four pieces for individual pizzas (or eight for smaller pizzas) and roll out into disks until about ¼ inch thick, or much thinner if a thin base is preferred. If making one large pizza, keep the dough as one piece and roll to a similar thickness.

Roasted Garlic & Olive-Oil Mash

PREPARATION TIME: 10 minutes | COOKING TIME: 40 minutes | SERVES: 4

1 whole garlic bulb
1 pound 5 ounces floury
    baking potatoes, peeled
    and cut into medium
    pieces
1 tablespoon extra-virgin
    olive oil
kosher salt and freshly
    ground black pepper

Preheat the oven to 350°F. Wrap the garlic bulb in foil, place on a baking sheet and roast for 40 minutes. Remove from the oven and let cool.

Put the potatoes in a saucepan, cover with water and bring to a boil. Simmer until cooked and tender, about 20 minutes. Drain off the water and put the pan back on the heat for a few minutes to evaporate any remaining water. Mash the potatoes until smooth.

Slice off the top of the garlic bulb and squeeze the garlic flesh into the potatoes. Add the olive oil and seasoning, and mix well. Serve hot.

Celery-Root Mash

PREPARATION TIME: 10 minutes | COOKING TIME: 20 minutes | SERVES: 4

1 pound 5 ounces celery root, peeled and cut into small pieces
4 tablespoons butter
kosher salt and freshly ground black pepper

Put the celery root in a saucepan, cover with water and bring to a boil, then simmer until cooked and tender, about 20 minutes. Drain off the water and put the pan back on the heat for a few minutes to evaporate any remaining water. Add the butter, season to taste and mash to a fine purée. For a really fine purée, use a handheld blender. Serve hot.

Goat-Cheese Mash

PREPARATION TIME: 10 minutes | COOKING TIME: 20 minutes | SERVES: 4

1 pound 5 ounces floury baking potatoes, peeled and cut into medium pieces
6 ounces rindless goat cheese
4 tablespoons butter
kosher salt and freshly ground black pepper

Put the potatoes in a saucepan, cover with water and bring to a boil, then simmer until cooked and tender, about 20 minutes. Drain off the water and put the pan back on the heat for a few minutes to evaporate any remaining water. Crumble in the goat cheese and mash with the potatoes. Season and mix in the butter. Serve the mash hot.

Cooked Turkey

PREPARATION TIME: 5 minutes, plus 20 minutes to cool | COOKING TIME: 10 minutes | SERVES: 4

3 boneless, skinless turkey breast steaks, about 3½ ounces each
2 cups chicken stock

Put the turkey steaks in a saucepan, cover with the stock and bring to a boil. Reduce the heat to low and simmer, covered, until cooked through, about 10 minutes. Remove the pan from the heat and let the turkey cool in the stock. When cool, remove the turkey from the pan and tear into bite-sized chunks. Discard the stock (or keep for another recipe).

Index